Popular Capitalism

POPULAR CAPITALISM

JOHN REDWOOD

ROUTLEDGE

First published 1988 by Routledge
First published in paperback 1989
11 New Fetter Lane, London EC4P 4EE
29 West 35th Street, New York, NY 10001

Phototypeset in 10pt Baskerville by
Mews Photosetting, Beckenham, Kent
Printed in Great Britain by Billing & Sons Ltd, Worcester

British Library Cataloguing in Publication Data

Redwood, John
    Popular capitalism.
    1. Developing countries. Economic growth.
    Role of capitalism
    339.5'9172'4

ISBN 0-415-00114-5
ISBN 0-415-00115-3 (Pbk)

To John Templeton

Contents

Preface   vii

1. Democracy Breaks Out:
   The Long Road to Freedom   1

2. Freeing the Market:
   In the Shadow of Adam Smith   24

3. The Road to Ruin:
   The World in Hock to Bankers   46

4. Disencumbering the State:
   Privatisation on a Global Scale   71

5. Financial Technology for Recovery:
   Rescheduling, Debt Swap and the Rebuilding
   of the Banking System   93

6. Making a Market:
   The Growth of International Stock Exchanges   114

7. Unburdening the Entrepreneur:
   Tax Reform in Many Countries   133

8. Conclusion   145

Postscript   158

Index   171

Preface

Almost ten years have passed since the Brandt Report reminded the world just how divided it had become. The split between the rich northern nations and the poorer southern nations was thrown into relief during the 1950s and the 1960s when the richer countries grew rapidly. The poverty of the poorer countries worsened in the decade of the 1970s as they were often the main losers from the massive increases in the prices of oil and other commodities they needed to import.

The Brandt Report made many recommendations as to how the poorer countries could be assisted. The basic message was the obvious one. Only economic growth could bring them prosperity and that growth had to be generated within the poorer countries as they were introduced to new technology and new skills. The Report recognised that whilst food aid might be necessary when people were starving, it was much better to teach a man to grow wheat than to give him bread. The Report still saw the process of development in terms of one government helping another rather than the private sector playing an important role in developing the poorer economies.

Some seven years later when the world had been through a major banking crisis and when many Third World countries had discovered they did not have the resources to pay the interest on their debts, the Americans introduced the Baker Plan. The three essential points of the Baker Plan were: to permit additional lending to developing countries, to foster the growth of the private enterprise economy in those countries and to impose some controls and limits on state activities in an effort to curb inflation, cut budget deficits and return countries to financial prudence. The Baker Plan was seen as a hopeful message, for like Brandt and unlike the caricature of IMF advice in the intervening years, Baker accepted the need for growth in the developing countries as the answer to their poverty.

The idea of a structured north/south dialogue is unlikely to produce the results that all men of goodwill must seek. Structured conversations between the great and good of the richer and poorer countries can only go so far in promoting understanding or economic development. What the world is again beginning to admit is that the problems of the developing world are most likely to be solved by a multitude of contacts between rich and poor and by harnessing the spirit of enterprise both within the developing countries and from without as new overseas investors are attracted to these territories.

There is no more important task in the world today than that of giving some hope back to the poorer countries. This book demonstrates why so many government-to-government solutions in the past have failed. It also sets out a new financial technology as a way of harnessing private enterprise to the cause of mutual development. This same change of ethos is apparent in many developed countries. In a variety of territories state socialism is being rolled back and governments are seeking faster growth through freeing markets and releasing the private sector. The large privatisation programmes, debt swap, private project finance on a large scale, tax reform and small enterprise policies are on many agendas. The aim of all these policies is to promote wider prosperity and ownership. They come together as popular capitalism and are now sweeping the world. Not even the stock market collapse and professional worries about equity can stop the process. Only days after the damage to the London market, money was raised to press ahead with Eurotunnel using private equity. The wider background to the pursuit of popular capitalism is a belief in democracy itself. There are common strands in glasnost in the USSR, in the economic reforms in China and the spread of democracy into the eastern and western edges of Europe. The story of popular capitalism begins with the spread of democracy.

I would like to say a special thank you to people I have worked with in recent years who have helped me as I have developed the thoughts in this publication. My years as Head of the Prime Minister's Policy Unit enabled me to work with a team of highly talented people at Downing Street. Their enthusiasm and dedication was most impressive. The style we evolved for understanding problems and offering policy advice was a collective style based upon free-ranging discussion and a wish to probe behind the conventional answers.

The Prime Minister has a special place in this story as the first international leader prepared to try many of these ideas and to argue for them with vigour and determination.

I am especially grateful to Oliver Letwin who joined me from the Downing Street Policy Unit at N.M. Rothschild and Son. He helped me set up N.M. Rothschild's international privatisation and financial service. Within 18 months of establishing it, we had seven government clients worldwide outside the United Kingdom. Given our joint political interests in the UK we never worked on a United Kingdom assignment. Oliver enabled me to operate on a wide-ranging basis which gave me exposure to government financial problems in many differing territories.

My third thank you is to Richard Downer, once the Jamaican Prime Minister's adviser and now a senior partner of Price, Waterhouse in Jamaica. Richard was my first client for international privatisation advice and with him I had the privilege of setting up the Jamaican Privatisation Programme for their Prime Minister and introducing Jamaica to the technology of debt swap. It is in no small measure due to Richard and his fortitude and clarity of mind that Jamaica has been able to undertake a major privatisation programme and to demonstrate that a stock exchange could be developed in a relatively small country.

My fourth debt of gratitude is to the N.M. Rothschild and Son's debt-swap team. I always believed that debt swap could be linked to privatisation to produce a non-inflationary way of converting debt into equity. The N.M. Rothschild debt-swap team, who have carried out many transactions in the regular, commercial debt-swap market, gave me insight and knowledge of the techniques of debt swapping which were invaluable when I came to introduce the technology to Jamaica.

My final and biggest debt of gratitude is to my family who had to live with two years of an exhausting schedule spending much time out of the country on international business, a three-week election campaign and then the writing of this book. Without their forbearance and support it would not have been possible.

1

Democracy Breaks Out: The Long Road to Freedom

Around the world there are important stirrings for freedom. The decade of the 1980s has seen signs of reversal in the strides towards Marxist tyrannies or military regimes. In the 1950s, 1960s and 1970s the world was gripped by an enthusiasm for state solutions. In the liberal West there were people who felt that maybe Marxism and authoritarian government was a good combination for forcing the pace of growth in Third World countries. Whilst those same liberal critics would have been the first to have cried out had anyone attempted to limit their own liberties in their own safe Western democracies, they were, none the less, prepared to argue that the economy of a poor country might be better served by a strongly centralised government which did not brook opposition. They argued that inequalities and poverty were so atrocious in some developing countries that only if the state took central direction of many industries and of agriculture, fixed the prices, and itself attempted to legislate the distribution of incomes, would things improve at all. This dangerous flirtation with Marxist tyranny had the desired effect. In many parts of the Pacific, Africa and Latin America, governments of the left took power and exercised that power with draconian firmness.

It was all too easy for this to produce an equal and opposite reaction. The natural antidote to the threat of Marxist takeover, or to Marxist government itself, was a short, sharp, violent *coup* by the armed forces. Those people on the right were able to claim that democracy was too weak or feeble to withstand the pressures of this new move towards Marxism, backed as it often was by liberal Western thinking. They argued that they should take control of the society through the army and attempt to demonstrate from the right that the speed of development could be improved and the distribution of incomes made more equal under military control.

It is but a short step for an elected government in a country with no long democratic tradition to move from believing that there are important national secrets that need defending by regulating the press, to taking a more embracing view of the desirability of limiting press freedom. It is then possible to go from placing constraints on journalists to closing down individual newspapers or television stations that are hostile to the 'national' cause. It might then be thought desirable, for commercial as well as for propaganda reasons, to nationalise the television or the radio channels. If the government is making progress but is still subject to the criticism of opposition politicians and of others outside the parliamentary process, why not start limiting the activities of the opposition? In the first instance the limitations may only be imposed on extra-parliamentary protests, demonstrations or things that may result in violence. It might then be possible to move from this to the position where it is even better to close down opposition within parliament itself. Why not dispense with the services of a factious and disruptive parliament when the cause of growth and income equality might dictate that the government, which knows best, should take the necessary powers?

This kind of thinking could turn democracies into single-party states and countries with a free press into highly censored societies. The problem was that this outbreak of petty left-wing tyrannies around the world did not seem to generate the faster growth or the greater justice that the liberal commentators in the West thought would naturally follow. Far from it. In many an African state the debts piled up, the injustices and the income inequalities grew larger and the economies failed to take off. At times the harvest failed and famine prevailed. At times civil wars broke out between competing factions or diversionary wars were started with neighbouring states. Disease, famine, dirt and poverty ground down the subject populations. The governments managed to distance themselves from these conditions by retaining control of the main avenues of power in the state and by ensuring that those at the top lived well. Ethiopia is a living indictment of this system.

In Latin America the experience of alternation between Marxism and military regimes similarly ensured that debts piled up, debt upon debt, high inflation rates remained the order of the day and the economies failed to exploit the natural resources and advantages with which they are endowed. Western bankers were all too willing to lend, believing sovereign risk was low risk. It turned out not only that democracy failed but that the economies failed as well.

It should not come as any surprise that the eclipse of freedom in the political sphere also generates economic difficulties. Looking back at the successful history of the Western nations where, by and large, economies have flourished and people have become ever more prosperous, an inescapable link between economic liberalism and economic advance emerges. It was the Dutch who dominated the seventeenth century. Their success, out of all proportion to the size of their population, or even to the breadth of their economic base, was centred fairly and squarely upon free trade. It was the success of Amsterdam as an entrepôt for every kind of business and merchandise, and the strength of the Dutch trading economy, open to all the influences and products of the new world and the old, that caused the Dutch to prosper so mightily.

In the nineteenth century, when Great Britain was at the peak of its imperial fame, and when it was the most prosperous country and the most powerful nation in the world, it too based its success upon the principles of free trade. The great ports of Liverpool, London and Bristol were open to the trade of the world and the British currency was not only freely convertible into others but was the mainspring of world commerce. In the twentieth century, when American power has come to dominate, that too has been based upon the economic freedom that a free trade area covering over 220 million people in its domestic market can provide. The Americans similarly have financed world trade, issued a freely convertible currency and have been open to all the influences that various types of immigration and the import of new ideas can bring.

Whilst democracy of itself may not be enough to guarantee Western style prosperity, tyranny rarely produces the enterprise that generates high incomes and wealth. In India, for example, under a democratic regime, famine has been eliminated and the drive out of poverty has begun, but the freedom to vote for socialism has hindered part of its industrial growth. A society maybe free but have a deep seated hostility to prosperity.

Yet this simple message, that economic freedom and political freedom or toleration often go hand in hand, was deliberately ignored by many developing countries. In this they were assisted by Western governments, keen to lend money government to government and to back state solutions to social and economic problems. And, above all, they were assisted by that strand of liberal Western thinking which maintained that political liberty was fine

3

for the West but was a dispensable extra as far as the developing world was concerned. Everyone came to believe in the powers of the enabling state. If we expand the state into transport it will enable everybody to travel by bus. If we extend the state into the water industry, it will mean everyone has a clean water supply. But so often the enabling state became the disabling state. The state imposed controls and regimentation. It took away incentive and prevented people from developing the kind of country and the kind of business they wished to develop. The state developed its own deadweight and its bureaucracy became one of the main impediments to faster economic growth.

It was against this spirit of the age that the stirrings of the 1980s first occurred. In Europe itself democracy was not safe on the peripheries in the west and the east. Whilst the French and the British had well-established democracies, and whilst the Italians and the Germans after World War II were keen to re-establish democratic traditions and live down the excesses of the reign of the dictators, the same was not true in the Iberian peninsula or in the eastern Mediterranean.

In Spain the 1970s saw the first important movement towards freedom, which was a harbinger of the 1980s. The Franco regime came to an end, and the combined skills of an intelligent constitutional monarch, and the flourishing political parties which developed, ensured that Spain, at least for the time being, became safe for democracy.

A freer press was allowed. Greater diversity and choice became available in television, radio, magazines and newspapers. Opposition parties set up in business and elections were held that were free and enabled the people to choose the government of the country. Over the last ten years democracy has been greatly strengthened in Spain and it is maturing rapidly. At the same time Spain has begun to compare with the Western community of nations in terms of prosperity and economic growth. It has joined the European Economic Community, which has assisted in opening Spain to more foreign influences. It has begun to relax its draconian exchange controls and to be more open to outside pressures on investment, products and standards of service. Madrid today is a much more modern city than ten years ago and the vitality and the thought which can come from political democracy and diversity is an important part of that story.

Its neighbour, Portugal, has taken longer to wake up from its authoritarian slumbers and begin the process of modernising itself, to bring it nearer the forefront of Western European nations. But it is encouraging that 1987 saw another free election in Portugal and that the Portuguese people have this time chosen to elect a firm majority government of the centre left, backing a programme of economic liberalism. The Portuguese have expressed through their ballot boxes a wish to modernise and to be part of the new trend around the world freeing enterprise to get on with the job of making their society more prosperous. The Iberian peninsula, at least for the time being, looks much safer for democracy than at any time in the twentieth century and, as a direct result, it is making rapid strides towards becoming part of the Western community of prosperous free nations.

Turning to the east of Europe, the picture is less certain. Both Greece and Turkey would claim, in their separate ways, to be making strides towards genuine democracy. But just how far can we believe in these movements? In Turkey there were elections in the 1970s/80s under Prime Minister Ozal, but a large number of politicians were excluded from them on the grounds that they were too disruptive to the state. The presence of the military is still clear on the streets in Turkey and in the government buildings. Whilst it is claimed that opposition and criticism in the newspapers is welcome, there is every sign that most of the information circulating in the Turkish press and society is sympathetic to the government. Turkish people do not yet know how far they can go in voicing dissent or encouraging true debate about ideas. It may be that Turkey is now on the road to democracy, but it needs to be freer with its civil liberties and more open in its attitude to the range of political opinions that can be channelled both through the press and on the hustings before it can truly claim to have rejoined the democratic community. It is encouraging that a narrow majority voted for the return of the excluded politicians to the electoral process in 1987.

In Greece there has been a similar problem in the relationship between the democratic state and the military. There have been times when the military have seized power and other times when it has looked possible that a proper democracy could be rebuilt. We are in one of those phases where democracy seems to be winning through, but there is still a long way to go.

The rest of Europe seems free for democracy. In the Scandinavian countries, in the central European states west of the communist bloc, in the Iberian peninsula and now perhaps in the eastern Mediterranean, democracy is again in the ascendancy. Since World

5

War II a period of true democracy in Germany, Italy and France has coincided with a tremendous renaissance of their economies. The growing prosperity of western Europe has been made to look even more startling in contrast with the drab, second-rate performance of the eastern European states, firmly under the grip of their Russian masters. In Scandinavia prosperity has resulted from freedom and democracy and has co-existed with welfare socialism.

In Latin America democracy has been in trouble. In 1983 Argentina decided to return to free elections and to civilian government. The fall of the military regime was the direct result of their incompetence and bungling. The Generals had allowed the economy to deteriorate as so many Argentinian governments had done. High inflation, high debt, low standards of production and a failure to industrialise quickly were hallmarks of the Argentinian experience throughout most of the post-war period. Under the generals and the military chiefs this became an art form. In an effort to divert criticism and attention, the military chiefs embarked upon the Falkland Islands adventure. Flagrantly violating international law and the niceties of international diplomacy, they hoped that by capturing an island which so many Argentinians believe should be rightfully theirs, they would succeed in bolstering popular support for the regime. The humiliating military defeat led almost directly to the fall of the regime and to the incarceration of some of its leading figures. The subsequent free elections and the resumption of the democratic process was encouraging. But we must recognise that Argentina will always be unstable until democracy becomes the norm and until the democratic politicians begin to harness the energies of the people. The democratic government needs to tackle some of the huge economic problems inherited from its military predecessors.

Argentina's near neighbour, Brazil, has had a similar difficulty in restoring democracy after a military regime. Although many in the West feel that the return to democracy in Brazil is a triumph, delivering a left-of-centre government, it is important to understand that all is not well in that country. The military is very much in evidence. It ham-fistedly intervenes in much of life and there is not yet a sufficient tradition of dissent, opposition and lively criticism to be able to say that Brazilian democracy is alive and well. We cannot doubt the intentions. The endless drafting and redrafting of constitutions often stumbles over just how far and how fast the leading players wish to go, but there is general agreement that the direction should be towards more democracy. The problem is the vested interests, the tradition of army intervention in political life and the economic difficulties which beset any government of Brazil as it tries to establish itself for more than a few months. Brazil's claim to be a democracy rests upon the election of a president and upon the endless debates it is now having about the establishment of a new constitution. Meanwhile, the economy remains in a parlous state. Like Argentina, almost its neighbour, the debts have piled sky-high, inflation is nearly always present and the economy has never realised its enormous potential. Against this background democracy may prove unstable.

In the Pacific, the moves toward democracy have been more resolute and more dramatic than they have in Latin America. Leaving aside the remarkable Philippines revolution, there have been important stirrings for freedom in Korea, and in China itself.

South Korea was one of those rare examples of the conjunction of political tyranny with a rapid advance to prosperity. President Chun was used to ruling without opposition. The opposition parties have always been fragmented and have had to be careful about what they said. They effectively played no part in the political process. But in June 1987 the people of South Korea, despite their prosperity, started rioting. President Chun had thought that he would be able to pass the baton on to his chosen successor in the time-honoured way, without there being any effective competition for the post. The people felt otherwise. They wanted an election in which there was a genuine choice between the different opposition parties and Mr Chun's party. The riots multiplied and forced the President into meeting and talking to Mr Kim, the main opposition leader. This was an unprecedented departure in South Korean politics. The resulting long meeting, which remains largely unreported as far as the world is concerned, was a humiliation for Mr Chun and a feather in the cap, not only of Mr Kim, but also of possible South Korean democracy. In August 1987 the riots were followed by big strikes. The opposition parties were keen to foment the industrial unrest and the strikers signed up behind a programme of more democracy, especially more democratic trade unions with more clout. Now that the people of South Korea have tasted power by forcing the President on to the defensive, it is likely that there will be further strides towards a more genuine democracy in South Korea.

Of all the moves towards democracy the two that are most fascinating are those within the two largest communist countries, China and the Soviet Union. Chinese and Russian communisms have been very different since their inception. China has always been less centralised and more prepared to experiment than Russia. The origins of Mr Deng's farming policy in 1978 lay in the great famine of 1960 when 25 million died because of the failure of the collective farming system. In 1978 Deng's revolution stripped the commune officials of their powers and effectively established private farming. Each farmer rents land which becomes more or less his own and can be passed on to his children. The problem with the reform has been that it has created 180 million small farms, with an average size of only three quarters of an acre. None the less this reform did improve the state of agriculture.

Russia has been more reluctant to undertake these moves and has suffered in consequence. In both Russia and China one of the main problems has been the overriding of the price system and the eclipse of effective markets. For all their imperfections, markets remain the best of the known mechanisms for bringing together buyers and sellers. Price remains the only way of tempting more supply to prevent scarcity or reducing supply to prevent over-production. In the liberal West, because many people for much of the time do not like the answers that the markets throw up, there has been a temptation to forget this basic truth. This has been nowhere more obvious than in the twistings and turnings of political and economic commentators in the West on the subject of oil. When oil leapt up from $2 a barrel to $12 a barrel and then again from $12 a barrel to nearer $30 a barrel, the commentators all wrote about the impending end of the industrialised world as we know it and the fact that energy was going to run out within 15 or 20 years. Whenever the oil prices dipped back again to $20 or $10, or even below $10 in the mid-1980s, articles were written about the glut of oil and the way the economy was going to be wrecked by the cheap oil flooding the world.

These commentators are falling prey to the emotions of the marketplace in its most speculative phases. For what they are witnessing is something which disproves all their fears. When the price of oil rises sharply, people cut back on its use. They find substitutes. They insulate their houses and their factories and their shops. They reduce their lighting or find ways of re-using heat that was being wasted. They make a substantial investment in conservation. At the same time that the consumer is busy cutting back, the producer is busily expanding. Once the oil price goes up people discover that there is more oil in less hospitable parts of the world which, at a price, they can go and exploit. They discover that, at a price, there are substitutes for oil. There are the tar sands and shales around the world where oil can be squeezed out if enough money is spent. There is the prospect of building a very large nuclear generating capacity in many different countries. There is the possibility that wind, tide and sun power, all renewable forms of energy, can become economic as the oil price rises. People dust down the projects for lignite-fired power stations, barrages across rivers, more hydro-electricity, experimentation with capturing the rays of the sun and a host of other exciting ideas.

Once the oil price falls the reverse happens. Many businesses, countries and individuals become more relaxed about burning oil and it is less worthwhile to spend money on conservation. At the same time the oil companies have to reduce the number of rigs that are drilling for oil in frontier regions, companies thinking of alternative energy sources start scrapping their plans or cutting back their funding and governments themselves, swayed by the prevailing tide of opinion, put the whole subject on the back burner.

These simple truths have been forgotten by some commentators in the liberal West who insist that there will be an energy crisis which can, in fact, never take place if there is a market. Markets have been deliberately eradicated by the communist regimes in China and Russia but the price of wiping out markets has been to damage both the economic and the moral structure of the countries concerned. The damage to the economic structure is visible to the naked eye for anyone who reads the figures or visits China and Russia. There are queues in the shops. The shops have insufficient goods for the customers. Many of the products that the West takes for granted are simply not available. People are not allowed to leave the country freely with money to spend in the West. There are stringent foreign exchange controls and there are often two- or three-tier markets, with different types of goods on offer to the party faithful or for foreigners, as their foreign exchange is needed when they do come as tourists or visitors.

The Russians and the Chinese found it difficult to feed their people during the collective farming period. China was forced into radical reforms, scrapping many of the state communes, whilst Russia has soldiered on. At every party congress the leadership has to make new pleas for better production. In consequence Russia has had to depend to a great extent on imported American grain to feed its people. The Russian and the Chinese industrial systems are at different stages of development but both, compared with the industrialised high-tech West and Japan, are backward.

The moral damage is in many ways as significant. For what happens when markets are eradicated is that they spring up illicitly.

Whatever socialist theory may say about human nature, the fact is that people have more incentive to work if they are going to get a direct benefit as a result. The back gardens, the small farms, the small enterprises of China and those that are allowed to survive in Russia have always been many times more efficient than the large state enterprises. A surprising amount of market garden produce, so important in the modest diets of eastern Europe and the Soviet Union, comes from the free enterprise activities of the market gardeners and the domestic gardeners of the communist bloc. Western clothes, records, tapes and books are contraband. They can be traded for high prices by those willing to take the risk.

Russian society demonstrates the impact on the human spirit that too conscious a pursuit of equality of outcome can have. The more talented people in the society are directed in one of four ways. Some decide that the human spirit cannot be as tied down and controlled as it is in the Soviet Union and they become the literary or political dissenters. Few survive. Many end up in labour camps or worse and a few come across to the West to achieve a better life. It is an irony that they are often welcomed in the West by the very people who believe the Western system is rotten and would like it to emulate some aspects of communist egalitarianism.

The second group go in the opposite direction and exercise their skills and their ambitions to get to the top of the party-dominated Russian state. They can thus achieve a level of material comfort and satisfaction far higher than the average Russian. For although Russia worships egalitarianism in all the speeches and rhetoric, it is in practice a deeply divided society, where those who get to the top of the party apparatus gain great privileges for themselves in terms of access to flats, houses, cars and consumer goods that others cannot buy, even if they had the money.

The third route is to become fatalistic. The talented Russian who has not made it in the party apparatus, and who is left working for one of the large state industries or collective farms, may decide that it is better to go for a quiet life. Many individuals lack edge or enthusiasm and many more turn to drunkenness or to other simple solaces.

The fourth route is to bring enterprise from beneath regardless of the hostile culture. You cannot abolish markets. Wherever more than a few people are gathered together in a community they will start trading with each other. They may have to do it illegally, it may be done by means of barter rather than for money, but trade they will. Testimony to this is the growing strength of the small enterprise farming and industrial sector.

It is interesting that China's economic structure is not nearly as ossified as that of the Soviet Union. In support of this contention the World Bank has recently published figures showing the size distribution of industrial enterprises. Table 1.1 compares China with Hungary, an example of just how far state domination and centralisation can go, and with South Korea and Japan, at the upper end of the range of free economies with a host of small enterprises. The significance of the figures for China is that they show just how small a proportion of total enterprises are represented by firms employing more than 243 people. It is in this band of larger sized firms that most of the large state enterprises are to be found. It is for this reason that in Hungary they account for 65 per cent of the total.

Table 1.1: Size differentiation of firms

No. of Employees	China 1982	Hungary 1981	South Korea 1981	Japan 1972
5–33	59.2	2.2	70.6	80.2
33–75	19.5	4.8	14.4	10.7
75–189	12.2	18.7	9.2	6.1
189–243	8.5	9.2	1.5	0.8
243 +	0.6	65.1	4.3	2.2

Source: *The Economist*

In China there is a growing awareness that following the relative success of free enterprise farming, something similar has to be done to invigorate the industrial sector and to encourage the new industrialisation which is going on apace. In industry people are beginning to experiment with socialist joint stock companies. This means that shares are owned by institutions controlled by the Communist Party. Even more interesting are the experiments with management and employee buy-outs, a style of privatisation which has attractions for socialist states and free enterprise alike. *The Economist* recently gave an example from Shaanxi Province. In this province the Chang'an electronic products factory which manufactured the metal boxes needed to contain many electronics assemblies, went into loss in 1983. A 29-year-old manager and local Communist Party secretary decided to issue Yuan bonds in equal numbers to each of the villagers. In return for the bonds the villagers gave away their rights in the factory and passed the assets to the managers and employees. Since then an annual dividend has been paid and the management has been fully responsible for the conduct of the business. A further 650,000 Yuan was raised through new share sales and by 1986 the factory made a profit of 550,000 Yuan a year. This is an impressive achievement. It is a good profit turnround for business on traditional employee buy-out principles, rebuilding morale and involving the local community as sleeping partners by issuing bonds and raising new capital from them.

China is reopening stock markets and is allowing more and more sales to take place in free markets rather than through the state shops. The state price system now poses a significant political problem to the Chinese authorities. For years the Chinese public have enjoyed stable prices in the state shops. This is important, as it was a wild inflation in the closing years of the old regime that was amongst the most important factors enabling the Communists to take power. Communists delivered their promise to restore and maintain price stability at the expense of choice and freedom.

It is true that the prices in the shops have stayed stable, but there have been chronic shortages of many goods. People often have to queue, or simply cannot buy what they want at all. Planned production has never been as centrally controlled as in Russia but still a large number of difficulties have arisen without a price signalling system to increase supply when demand is strong, or to cut supply when demand is weak. As a result, a parallel market is springing up. Many of the basics can still be bought in state shops and the prices are still fairly well controlled, but the typical Chinese housewife is now buying more and more things from the private marketplace where prices are much higher but where the choice and range of goods is also much wider than in the state shops.

The reformers in China are having a difficult time. The old guard does not like the idea of restoring market powers and, as they see it, market prices. But the reformers are out to limit the influence of the state planning committees and to increase the power of managers and the impact of prices. Each industrial factory is to be an accounting unit and is to be responsible for funding its own development and answerable to its bond financiers or shareholders. There is rapid growth of industry through a network of rural workshops which have many of the characteristics of free enterprise businesses. Markets are being actively encouraged and the price system is being brought in by the back door. As China gets more prosperous, that prosperity will be driven by a whole clutch of new private enterprise businesses, often financed on the back of the savings and profits of the free enterprise farming that started the revolution in the late 1970s and early 1980s.

Mikhail Gorbachev faces an altogether tougher task in the Soviet Union. By now most people in the West have heard the words *glasnost* and *perestroika*, meaning a better spirit of openness and criticism, and restructuring. What is often not realised is the enormity of the task facing Gorbachev and the fundamental changes which his speeches envisage. He is well aware of the shortcomings of Soviet society and the resulting economy. His speeches are full of criticisms of what is going on. For example, his recent criticism of the Communist Party of Armenia: 'A totally unjustified tranquillity is being shown in the republic. There are no standards with regard to personnel, and no effective efforts are being made against bribery, profiteering and protectionism.' His comments on Gorky are just as harsh: 'Many vitally important issues are tackled there in an unsatisfactory way, the powerful potential of the region is not duly utilised. The social sphere and the agrarian sector of the economy are developing weakly.'

Much of what was wrong with Russian society was summed up for Mikhail Gorbachev by the extraordinary event of the West German light plane flown by Rust landing in Moscow's Red Square. As he said, in his speech to the CPSU central committee in June 1987:

> It reminds us once again how strong and tenacious the negative trends (which were exposed by the April plenary meeting of the Central Committee and by the 27th Congress of the party) turned out to be in our society, and even in the army.
>
> This emphasises the need to enhance vigilance, to act still more resolutely, to strengthen discipline, to raise the degree of organisation, to enhance responsibility and improve performance everywhere and at all levels. (Quotes from M. Gorbachev are from *Soviet News*, July 1987, published by the Press Department of the Soviet Embassy in London)

Gorbachev has in mind a widespread reform. He knows that in order to improve performance he needs to instil a sense of responsibility and duty at the business and unit level. He knows as well that in a highly centralised and structured society like the Soviet Union the example has to come from the top. He has, in turn, to impress upon the Communist party bosses and the republics and regions of the massive, sprawling USSR, that he means business and that he intends to see the message taken right down to the level of the shop floor. His reforms abound with paradoxes. There is the paradox that he is trying to decentralise power by using the strongly centralised power at his disposal through the Communist Party. He is trying to encourage private enterprise and initiative and allow incentive and profit to play their part in a society which has to remain true to the doctrine of egalitarianism which has permeated all political discussion ever since the Revolution. He has to appeal to the legendary figures of communism like Lenin and Marx himself as being exponents of a kind of free enterprise socialism, accenting all the time the things in their messages which give some credence to his view that the true development of socialism from here rests upon the injection of a substantial element of democracy, freedom and free enterprise. But he should not be criticised for his illogicalities or his paradoxes. After all, religion abounds with paradox but this does not necessarily mean it is false. We should instead understand the enormity of the task that faces him and examine in detail the way this craftsman of the political art is going about refashioning a whole society stuck in its ways and failing to compete with the West in the way in which he wishes.

Gorbachev himself has set it out well in his speeches:

> The revolutionary transformations in society have brought to the fore the contradiction between the demands for renewal, creativity and constructive initiative, on the one hand, and conservatism, inertia and selfish interests on the other.

> The imbalance between the growing vigour of the masses, and the still-surviving bureaucratic manner of activity in most diverse fields and attempts to free the renewal drive is one of the manifestations of this real contradiction.

> Overcoming this contract requires prompt and resolute measures — in personnel policy and in the assertion of new approaches and norms of party, state and public life.

> What does the political bureau regard as the most effective means of solving this contradiction? The answer is clear cut and definite — the extensive development of democracy.

> Today, and this is again proved by life, it is the command

and administrative forms of managing society that put a break
on our movement. Democratic and *only* democratic forms are
capable of imparting a mighty acceleration to it.

This is indeed a mighty agenda. Critics in the West will say that
so far it does not amount to much. The idea that there should be
a choice of candidates in Soviet elections within the Party does not
mean that we are about to witness the blossoming of a two- or three-
party state. Yet these critics underestimate the significance of
offering any kind of choice between personalities within this highly
centralised controlled mass. If people are allowed a choice of candidates within the Communist Party, maybe there will also be a
divergence of views about what is the true line of communist
development. Is it possible that Mikhail Gorbachev could, through
his hesitant steps towards free elections, trigger off some genuine
debate and discussion within the Communist Party itself, which
will provide the challenge and the stimulus he is seeking? Is it also
the case that his elections to the top posts in the Communist Party
might succeed in removing a whole generation of elderly Communist
Party officials whom he clearly despises? These are the people he
sees standing in the way of reform and the enthusiasm and generation of new ideas that he believes Soviet society so desperately needs.
Is it true that he has been finding more traditional and less pleasant
ways of getting rid of his rivals? Could the elections begin to do
the job for him?

In the economic sphere Gorbachev is trying to inculcate a series
of new attitudes. Individual enterprises will have to account for all
their costs and he wishes to see them become self-financing. He
wishes to see flexible remuneration geared to results or a kind of
profit-sharing. As he said in a speech when he welcomed 'the first
steps to introduce principles of cost accounting and assert such principles of labour remuneration under which it is linked entirely with
end results'.

He is well aware of the need to increase incentives at all levels.
He took fortune into his hands when he started to attack the Russian
doctrine of equality:

It appears to be obvious that equality does not mean levelling.
But in practice we often got just that. The tendency towards
levelling persisted tenaciously. It generated sponging attitudes,
negatively influenced the quality and quantity of work and
reduced incentives to increase productivity.

He wishes to see every encouragement given to creative highly productive work and to talent. He also wishes to see idle, inefficient, drunken and incompetent people dealt with severely.

As Gorbachev gradually reforms the Party by changing personnel, he is also keen to see that decisions taken are followed up and implemented. In the Russian bureaucracy, large as it is, things solemnly decided by senior officials in the Party, or by the Congress itself, are often not followed up or implemented at all. Gorbachev intends to tighten up on all of this.

In the industrial restructuring, one of the most important tasks is to see that the goods produced are actually wanted and in demand. Gorbachev inherits an industrial organisation which makes things because they have always been made and fails to make other things, despite the fact that people would like to buy them. Gorbachev is trying to enshrine the customer into the economic body politic and trying to force industry to change so that it is better geared to the needs and demands of individual people.

He has a great sense of urgency in what he is saying.

> Firstly, we have already lost years and decades. Secondly, it may so happen that there will be no 'beautiful tomorrow' if one does not work today by the sweat of one's brow, changing the way of thinking, overcoming inertia, and mastering new approaches.

He is keen to see as much land as possible given over to individuals and families as he knows that their gardening and farming is so much more productive. He has been told there is a shortage of available land to do this. His reply is that either there is no such shortage or in those areas where there is, land should be given from collective and state farms to the new farming families and the farming enterprises. He is trying to bring in a family contract system of farming which can harness the efficiencies of free enterprise to a greater extent than the state collectives. As he himself says: 'First of all, what is needed is a person infinitely interested in the results of his work, and responsible for it.'

His philosophy is backed up at all times by a number of practical examples. This passage reveals how he is trying to go back to some important prior source of Marxism and at the same time, link it to a real life example in the current Soviet reform programme:

> We have long tried to manage the economy on the basis of

enthusiasm, and at times by decree. But we used to forget about Lenin's precepts that the growth of production can be ensured on the basis of personal interest, material incentives and with the help of enthusiasm.

It is significant that the first members of intensive work collectives in Nobosibirsk region, the Kozhukhov brothers from the Bolshevik collective farm in Ordynski district, say that what attracted them to this kind of collective was not only high wages but, in no smaller degree, independence, the realisation of their human significance, and pride that they do the necessary kind of work.

Gorbachev is saying that the ideological background to his enthusiasm for free enterprise farming is quite sound as he claims Lenin's parentage for it all. He is also saying that Russians, ordinary Russians, will respond to the twin pulls of more money and a greater degree of independence and responsibility in their work. The current state of Russian agriculture is such that Gorbachev bemoans the fact that over half all rural families fail to keep any cows and a third keep no livestock at all. Rural dwellers go to the food store to buy food in exactly the same way that urban dwellers do. His contract farming system is designed to put this right, with rural dwellers growing for themselves and growing a surplus by being much more efficient than the collective farms that used to employ them.

Gorbachev's task stretches across the whole economy. It is not only agriculture that needs a bomb under it. Housing too is very unsatisfactory. And the consumer goods shortage is something which worries him deeply. Listen again to his own words:

> Just look how many facts indicate that the population is poorly provided even with goods which are in ample supply. And if one adds that there is no due order in many institutions and enterprises of trade, that service standards are low, that there are many queues because the number of shops themselves is insufficient, and that the operating schedules in the sphere of trade and service are not always subordinated to the working and living mode of the population of towns and countryside, it becomes understandable why their work evokes criticism so often.

Gorbachev notes that a private service sector is developing, even the Central Statistical Administration admits in its report that substantial private service activities are being undertaken for payment, to make up for the deficiencies in service of so many of the state enterprises.

Gorbachev is trying to get all his officials to understand that democracy applies to them. It means that they have to consult with public opinion and encourage democratic discussion before taking any action. He welcomes the clash of opinions, criticism in the press and the other things that will flow from this decision. He encounters difficulties when openness leads to protest and riots. He then has to resort to the older tactic of army repression to settle the situation. Many of his colleagues in the Communist Party, protected for years from any searching criticism or opposition, are finding the going much more difficult. As he says:

> We regard people's control both as an efficient means for detecting new issues which demand urgent solution and as one of the most important forms of bringing the masses into the process of self-government, into running affairs of society of the state.

Gorbachev's task is mind-boggling in its proportions. There is a nice irony in one of the August 1987 issues of Pravda. In a passage on democracy the party paper says: 'Democratisation is not just a fine-sounding word, nor just a slogan of the day, but the very crux of the re-structuring drive which itself is only possible through the involvement of the broadest popular mases in every constructive initiative.' It goes on to talk about how the aim is to be achieved and says that

> both deputies (elected members of Soviets, or Councils) and officials give regular accounts of their work to work collectives and directly to the population, and that working people have the right to evaluate the performance of leaders, including the right to raise the issue of relieving of their posts those who have failed to cope with their duties or compromised themselves.

Readers are told that they have to tolerate dissent, think about using popular power to remove corrupt and bad party officials and make sure that Lenin's style of popular democracy and public opinion is brought to bear on the process of party, industrial and agricultural government. The irony is that this was undoubtedly planted in

Pravda by the central machine. The Gorbachev paradox is and will continue to be, that he can only decentralise and free people within the Soviet state by using the full panoply of his power at the very pinnacle of the central machinery.

It is too early to tell how far Gorbachev's resolution will carry him or the Soviet people. Many sceptical onlookers will say that his reforms will be window-dressing, or that he will be thwarted by the enormous entrenched vested interest which he faces. In comparison, the task that Margaret Thatcher took on in the United Kingdom looks mild and modest indeed. For Gorbachev has to change Soviet society from top to bottom, has to countenance new appointments or the change of personnel in thousands of Party and managerial posts around the country, and he has to give back to people a sense of independence and some control over their own destiny. He envisages a Soviet society in which popular opinion is expressed through the Party machine and where people can make limited choices from within the Party for the candidates whose views they like best. He envisages a world where there is a genuine exchange of opinions between managers and employees in the state enterprises, where there is a much bigger, thriving private service sector outside the state collectives with people running their own small businesses and, in agriculture, a contract farming system where individual families farm what is effectively their own land. It is, above all, the construction of a grand democracy which Mikhail Gorbachev says he has in mind. It is difficult to see why he should take such obvious risks in the current state of the Soviet Union unless he means business.

Gorbachev's enthusiasm for talks with Margaret Thatcher, for learning from her about the differences between the West and the East and the reasons why she does things the way she does, indicates a seriousness of intent which we would be wise not to underestimate. If Mikhail Gorbachev can stay alive politically and physically he is destined to become one of the all time great Soviet Union leaders. His reforms may succeed in modernising Russia in a way only surpassed or equalled by Peter the Great's. There are some remarkable similarities in the techniques used now by Mikhail Gorbachev and those displayed by Peter the Great. There are also some very interesting parallels between the forces that resisted Peter and the forces that now resist Mikhail Gorbachev. Where Peter the Great was primarily obstructed by the Orthodox church, Mikhail Gorbachev will be primarily obstructed by his own Communist Party. Both had to rely upon the loyalty of the armed forces and Mikhail Gorbachev has to make sure that the new generation of generals and marshals are people with whom he can do business and on whom he can rely.

At the other end of the world a different kind of revolution for democracy was led by Corazon Aquino in the Philippines. Corazon Aquino became a determined woman and transformed herself into an energetic and important politician following the murder of her husband under the Marcos regime. Her speeches prior to election, during the election campaign and after her historic victory are a moving testament to the determination of one woman to restore democracy in her country and to the bravery of that woman in providing a rallying point for the forces of freedom.

On 1 October 1985 Corazon Aquino looked forward to the possibility of removing the long running and well set dictator Marcos by democratic means. She said then:

> We are certain that Mr. Marcos has his back against the wall. Is it possible then to displace him without resorting to the use of violence and thereby triggering the cycles of instability and suppression that his removal seeks to avoid? . . . I am confident that a peaceful political solution still is possible. I base my confidence principally on four factors: first, the capacity of opposition parties to unite; second, the electoral militancy of the awakened Philippino; third, the moral leadership of the church; fourth, the reform movement in the military.
>
> I am confident that the opposition will unite under one candidate when the presidential elections are held.[1]

In this important statement Corazon Aquino sketched out the forces that could carry her to ultimate victory. At the time many disbelieved her. Marcos was in a strong position with the military behind him and he had the right to choose when to hold the elections.

Once the election was called and the campaign begun, support built up quite quickly. On 3 February 1986 Corazon Aquino, in one of the most moving political speeches that can ever have been made, spelt out what had been happening.

> I say to Mr. Marcos what Moses said to the cruel, enslaving Pharaoh — let our people go! The nation has awakened. I, like millions of Philippinos, look on this awakening as the dawning of a new day.

---

1. All quotes from 'People Power'

Less than two months ago I said yes to a million signatures that asked me to run; the people power phenomenon began and rallied around the widow of Ninoy.

The people are crying for change. Volunteers have bravely come forth in battalions. Even the poorest have offered gestures of support. And the women! They have cast caution to the winds to campaign and lead in the peoples' crusade. They are determined to prove that people power is mightier than all the men and money of the crumbling dictatorship. I have criss-crossed the length and breadth of the nation. I have travelled by air, by plane and by helicopter; I have travelled by land. I have seen the devastation wrought by a policy built on a mountain of lies.

I have seen the broken bodies of men, women, and children buried under promises of peace and progress. I have heard the anguished voices of the victims of injustice answered only by hypocritical pledges of retribution.

I have been kissed by the poorest of the poor, and have felt the warmth of their tears on my cheeks. I have been emboldened by the eager embrace of throngs determined to put an end to this regime.

I have heard them shout that I must win. I have been electrified by their every cry for freedom, and inspired by their every clasp of hope.

I cannot shut my ears to them. I cannot turn my back on them.

Cory Aquino's estimated electoral victory was turned into a modest defeat by all kinds of ballot rigging and malpractice. A long struggle ensued to get the answer righted and the people's wishes upheld. There were dramatic sights on the streets of Manila and the other principal towns of the Philippines. Rosaries, Catholic priests, nuns, women carrying flowers outfaced the tanks and the military might of the Marcos regime. People power took to the streets and made it clear in massive demonstrations that they thought Cory Aquino had won and that Marcos should give way.

It was not until 24 February, more than a fortnight after the election, that the rebel troops succeeded in taking control of Channel 4 at exactly the point when Marcos was making a broadcast to try and calm people down, claiming that he was still in full control. Enough control was established for Cory Aquino to make her inaugural address as President of the Philippines Republic on that day, 24 February. She said:

It is fitting and proper that, as the rights and liberties of our people were taken away at midnight twenty years ago, the people should firmly recover those lost rights and liberties in the full light of day.

It took the brutal murder of Ninoy (her husband) to bring about the unity, strength, and the phenomenon of people power. That power, or Laks ng Bayan has shattered the dictatorship, protected the honourable military who have chosen freedom, and today has established a government dedicated to the protection and meaningful fulfillment of the people's rights and liberties.

We became exiled in our land — we, Philippinos, were at home only in freedom — when Marcos destroyed the republic fourteen years ago. Through courage and unity, through the power of the people, we are at home again.

Although President Marcos went through a similar inaugural ceremony, in the evening of the following day he left the country. Corazon Aquino had established her revolution. As she herself said, it was by no means certain that democracy would survive and flourish in the Philippines but its survival rested entirely upon her and her strength of character. Peoples' power, which had begun with the long silent file past at the funeral of Ninoy had been harnessed into a massive movement determined to restore freedom and rights to the Philippines people. The important defection of Minister Enrile and General Ramos gave Cory Aquino the party she needed and the power she required to fashion a political and even a military movement out of the naked belief of all those who took to the streets that Marcos' reign was over.

The display of Philippino people power was the most moving and most dramatic of all of the 1980s movements towards freedom. The South Korean street demonstrations are important and, in some ways, were modelled on the Philippino example. But they did not gain the same emotional prominence as this movement did in the Philippines, a desperately poor country, led by a woman whose husband had been murdered by the man she wished to depose. More than anyone else Cory Aquino came to represent the embodiment of the new march of democracy against tyranny. Important though the moves towards democracy may prove to be in China and in Russia, encouraging though it is that the Iberian peninsula has been won back for freedom, interesting though it may be that Argentina, Brazil and some other Latin American countries have made hesitant steps in the right direction, there is nothing to match the singular determination and the dramatic events that unfolded in January and February 1986 in Manila.

The worldwide movement towards democracy may peter out. In Fiji a military *coup* has at least temporarily overturned a democratic constitution. It will undoubtedly be subject to many twistings and turnings of fortune around the world. It would not be surprising to see the march to democracy in Brazil halted abruptly. In Argentina than is a precarious balance and in Chile, General Pinochet may not be forced in the direction in which events are currently moving. It may be that there is a counter-revolution in parts of the communist world and Cory Aquino herself could prove to be a transitory phenomenon in a state torn by what amounts to a civil war and in which the military is not entirely used to civilian style government.

None the less, enough has happened already to demonstrate three things. First, the democratic movement in the Third World has found, in the person of Cory Aquino, and in the demonstrations of people power, a role model as important as the passive resistance of Ghandi to the Raj in showing countries that they could become independent of Western domination. Second, there is amongst many peoples of the world, even amongst the poorest communities, an inner yearning for freedom which all dictators and Marxist regimes have to beware of. There are times when they can suppress it. There are times when the suppression can be effective for a long period. But there is always a small voice crying for freedom somewhere and there will come a time in many countries of the world where it can be amplified, as we have seen in several in the 1980s. Third, there is an understanding in the world today that economic success and greater equality have not resulted from the powerful tyrannies of the right or the left in the way in which those governments promised. So there is a new movement which believes not only in the need for freedom, civil liberty and political dialogue, but also understands that this can give rise to a liberal economics, a freeing of enterprise wich may be important in rebuilding or creating prosperity. These three basic considerations lie at the root of much of modern world politics. It is a foolish politician who ignores the march to freedom or who misunderstands the significance of the way people will continue to campaign for their liberties even in the most difficult circumstances.

2

Freeing the Market: In the Shadow of Adam Smith

In the world not only are there stirrings for democracy, but there is a major movement towards greater economic freedom. Capitalism, long out of fashion, is making a comeback. Marxism is on the defensive and on the retreat. Socialism in many countries of the world is having to be rethought. In those places where socialist and social democratic parties are prepared to embrace the new doctrines of economic liberalism they are showing signs of recovery or success. In those places where the conservative parties have been keen to grasp the idea of economic freedom they have been in the ascendency.

The new ideas behind the new politics are old ideas revisited. Markets are the most powerful mechanism for allocating resources. If a country is short of a given product or service the price of it has to rise. Then more people are prepared to produce it. If there is a glut then the price has to fall to reduce the amount of production or to increase the attractiveness to the customers. Competition is always better than a monopoly. For years private industries have gone about their business trying to establish cartels, arrangements, cosy agreements and monopolies themselves. At the same time governments have come to be one of the most important reasons why so much of industry worldwide is heavily monopolised and cartelised. It has been governments that have taken large industries into public ownership and have given them statutory or legal-based monopolies. It has been governments that have decided to subsidise, to rig prices, to restrict competition, to impose restrictions on imports or exports or foreign currency or borrowing, and have decided that they know better than the market place when it comes to making crucial investment decisions or in planning for the future.

In the process government has been pulled into a vicious cycle of ownership, subsidy, fudged decisions, bad investments, more subsidy, more fudges and bad decisions leading to the debilitation of the underlying industrial or commercial strength of the country. Governments gradually began to learn that owning and directing industry and commerce compromises their main task. For government should be the arbiters, the people above the factious disputes between industries, companies and individuals. Government should be the upholder of the law and the arbitrator in disputes over contracts. It is government's job to set a framework in which free trade can flourish in any given community. Government has to set down a law of contract, it has to defend people from theft or violence, it has to stand behind people and property, see that the law is properly enforced and make whatever regulations, legal changes or other arrangements are necessary as a result of free debate to adjust trading and competitive conditions to changing circumstances. It is very difficult to carry out this role fairly or with impartiality if at the same time government is acting as owner and manager of a whole series of assets.

How can a government form a fair judgement about how to treat private sector competitors on the margin of a large nationalised industry, when the nationalised industry is under financial pressure and the government itself has no more money to spend on it? How can the government represent the interests of the private sector competitors properly when all its information and most of the pressures upon it are coming from the nationalised industry that itself has everything to lose from successful private competitors? How can a government form a fair judgement on the economic wisdom of tariffs, subsidies or other interventions when it is itself the owner of a large chunk of the affected assets and when it is constantly being lobbied by the industry it claims to run? These and a number of other difficulties have cropped up as governments have confused the role of arbiter with the role of owner, director and manager.

On a wider canvas, we can see now that Marxism, for the time being, is on the retreat. The previous chapter has shown just what remarkable changes are under way in both China and Russia, particularly to restore the price mechanism and some free enterprise. This will not go unnoticed in the uncommitted developing world. Ten or fifteen years ago they might have been swayed by the belief that a strong centralised state could deliver the goods better and faster and that the loss of freedom, if it were a price, did not weigh heavily in the balance. They would now equally be swayed by the mounting evidence of the failure of Marxist economics and by its innate contradictions. It is by now apparent that, far from liberating the people and giving the people sovereignty in the way in which Marx envisaged, the state comes to dominate and the bureaucracy takes over. Instead of the state withering away, Marxist and socialist communities have become more and more dominated by bureaucratic apparatus and by a series of state institutions and controls that make the task of living a full and free life much more difficult.

It was Marx who argued that the inherent contradictions of capitalism would bring the system tumbling down. There are still people throughout the world eagerly awaiting the day when these innate contradictions will come careering through and the Western capitalist societies will end in crisis. These are the people who, every time GNP dips, or there is some faltering in trade, or inflation picks up, or the stock market declines, will look skywards and say that at last the promised land awaits. They foresee the collapse of capitalism in every downturn in the Dow Jones Index, and greet with glee any sign that the capitalist system is temporarily going to fail to deliver more and more prosperity. But many other people around the world are now looking at the real alternative on offer. Far from communism in practice offering a land of milk and honey where the state withers, where the people are enfranchised and empowered, where they have real choice and where prosperity expands, they are being served up a drab, dull, egalitarian utilitarianism, subjected to an overweening bureaucracy and party apparatus and forced to live well below the standards of living of the free West. The crowning irony has been that whilst Marxism has delivered a broad egalitarianism between most people in the society, at the expense of a much lower average standard of living, it has thrown up glaring anomalies as people have used the Party and bureaucratic apparatus to reward themselves much more highly in a variety of ways and to give themselves privileges to obtain goods and services that the others simply cannot acquire for love or money.

The innate contradictions of Marxism have always been more glaring than those that Marx thought he saw in capitalism. Marx was right that there are times when the capitalist system can engender a financial or a production crisis. There are times when people produce too many of the same thing. But capitalism has a way of dealing with it. As we have seen before, the price mechanism will, in the medium term, take care of the problem. Contrast that with Marxism where, if the state misplans nobody can bring it to account unless the party apparatus throws up a new *apparatchik*, and no-one can limit production errors until the bureaucratic and political process decides to change its mind. The innate contradictions of Marxism are legion. Over-production and under-production are all too likely in a state planned system. The mal-distribution of resources between weaponry and consumer goods, between consumption and investment is all too evident. The exclusion of the people from politics under the very system that is meant to enfranchise the working poor and the collapse of the egalitarian ideal under the usual pressures of vested interest favouritism are amongst the most obvious.

What then, are the new ideas of economic liberalism on offer? What are the old truths of Adam Smith or of Mandeville's "Fable of the Bees" that have suddenly been rediscovered?

The first is that reducing monopoly or liberalising an industrial or commercial sector is a way to encourage growth, new jobs, innovation, new services and lower prices. There have been many examples around the world of the successful withdrawal of monopoly rights. Take, for example, the case of the British inter-city bus industry. Most inter-city coach services were provided by the National Bus Company. The government decided to liberalise it by allowing new entrants to the market who could compete to provide services between the major cities of the country. At the time that this was undertaken the country warned that it would lead to a reduction in coach services. It was said that it might lead to an increase in the price of the service and the deterioration of its quality. The spectre of an important fabric of social service provision being irreparably damaged by the brute forces of competitive business was brought out into view.

The results of the liberalisation were the opposite. A large number of new service providers came forward. The fares fell by an average of one quarter. The service quality improved. A whole host of additions were made to existing services, including meals, newspapers, videos, toilet facilities and the like, provided during long coach journeys. The results of the improved service quality, the greater range of services on offer and the lower price was a huge surge in usage of the coach service. Within a year total use had gone up by 70 per cent.

This induced a virtuous circle. The lower fares brought in higher utilisation rates and more revenues. The businesses were therefore fairly profitable, whilst at the same time offering a better deal to the customer. There were problems with some of the early competitors, but the market took care of these, passing the assets on to someone else to manage, or inducing a change of business profile in the competing business until they found the right way of responding. The fact that National Bus held on to the lion's share of the market does not negate the importance of the liberalisation. Without the liberalisation National Bus would not have changed its management style and introduced so much better a deal for the customer.

The second type of activity is privatising. The idea of privatisation developed in London and now spreading worldwide is to encourage new private capital and new management styles into what were state run enterprises. Subjecting the business to the disciplines of the market means that it has to remunerate its capital, repay its debts and honour its interest charges, and adopt a commercial approach to all its ventures. Privatising, as this book will demonstrate, is now a worldwide phenomenon. Just as the New Zealand and several Caribbean governments are busily liberalising their economies, breaking monopolies and introducing new freedom to compete, so in 50 or 60 countries state assets are being returned to the private sector through public offers for sale or through the sale of assets to individuals and companies interested in exploiting them better.

The third way of spreading greater enterprise and economic freedom has been to develop big private projects through project finance or through venture finance where before the state would have run the activity. In the UK the Channel Tunnel project is an example of the type of infrastructure development that many years ago would naturally have been carried out by the government. Instead, a private company has been formed, shares have been issued and money raised, and substantial bank borrowings undertaken by the new company. The banks have as their security the asset of the tunnel under the English Channel and the revenues it will enjoy over many years as the prime method of communication between the UK and continental Europe. Many governments are now seeing the advantages of encouraging project financiers to find novel solutions to problems that before would have been state dominated and built with state debt. They are also seeing the advantage of building venture capital markets in their own country so that many ventures can now be undertaken with genuine risk capital, with the intermediation of savings through a market to plough into riskier ventures.

A fourth idea, which is spreading equally rapidly, is the establishment of private sector companies in areas of activity where before the nationalised industry was dominant or had a protective monopoly. The telecommunications industry is undergoing a major revolution worldwide. It is common for telecommunications to be organised on a nation by nation basis and for each nation to have entrusted its telecommunications to a single national carrier. The new technology is more diverse, permitting radio link competition to cable networks and permitting satellite competition as well. As a result, and as a consequence of deliberate liberalisation policies, there are now several countries in the world following the US lead of permitting new private businesses to set up in competition with the previous national monopoly enterprise. The policy began in the United States with the challenge to the Bell Company's monopoly of telephone services. Before long, GTE and MCI had taken a reasonable share of a large and growing market and had a substantial impact upon the tariff and service policy of the Bell monopoly.

The UK followed this path with the liberalisation of its telecommunications industry and the deliberate establishment of a private sector competitor, Mercury, which has the task of establishing a reasonable market share to make an impact on British Telecom's service and prices. Many countries worldwide are now considering or actually going down the same route. France is currently investigating the possibility of a second force communications company to challenge its own state monopoly business. In many developing countries deregulation coupled with the injection of new private capital through new companies into telephone monopolies is very much on the agenda. Similar things are happening in transport industries worldwide.

The fifth idea is to convert outstanding debt into equity. This can happen in many different ways. At its most simple, a company which is heavily indebted and in the state sector raises equity money from the market and some element of this new money is used to repay debt. At its most complicated, it entails a series of transactions enabling a heavily borrowed central bank to make local currency available to a new investor in return for cancellation of some foreign currency debt for that country. In a complicated series of transactions, the fact that the debt is no longer worth its face value is used both to give some benefit to the nation undertaking the process, and to the new investor.

The sixth element in economic liberalism is the rapid growth of stock markets. Many countries saw stock markets as at best an irrelevance, at worst an undesirable kind of casino which, if closed down, would probably improve the economic strength of the nation. There is now a much more mature understanding of the role that equity-raising capital markets have to play in development economics. Many countries worldwide wish to have a broader and deeper stockmarket. Some are beginning to learn from the British and the French experience that privatisation and other elements of economic liberalism can make an important contribution to the broadening and deepening of stock exchanges. The phenomenal strength and depth of the London market has been demonstrated by a twenty-fold increase in its equity capital-raising capacity in less than ten years. This enlargement has been powered by a switch in government financing from dept to equity and by the new marketing techniques pioneered to handle a very large privatisation programme.

The French, who had begun expanding their rather small equity market earlier, through the Loi Monory, are now discovering that privatisation is doing something similar to their stock market. Once a country has a reasonable sized stock market in relation to its GNP, it then has a new option for raising non-inflationary long-term risk capital for a variety of enterprises, and it becomes a useful adjunct to the policy of cutting state debt. There are also many countries worldwide where private sectors have been heavily debt financed. When interest rates rise and the currency shows instability, this can cause great problems to the commercial and industrial sector. Companies can go bankrupt because of their financing structures. The growth of a stock market gives a company another option and enables it to reduce its financial risks through cutting its interest charges by substituting equity for debt.

The seventh set of policies relate to the stimulation or encouragement of small business. We have already seen how important this is going to be in Chinese and even in Russian developments. Studies worldwide have shown that the small business sector produces more innovations and more new ideas per unit of research money spent, and also demonstrates that it is small business which usually has the flexibility to adjust to new markets and new conditions and to create the extra jobs that many societies require. Many countries are therefore looking at those areas of the world where small business has been strongest and are taking both liberalisation and economic stimulation measures to encourage the growth of a more virile small business sector.

The eighth area lies in taxation policy. In conjunction with the development of egalitarian liberal nostrums, and the belief that the state could provide for all, came a belief in heavily redistributive income tax. Taxation was placed more heavily on income rather than on spending or property; there was a trend towards higher and higher average and marginal tax rates in order to pay for the growing burden of state activity. There is a new spirit abroad which favours both lower average taxes and a switch from heavily redistributive income taxation to other forms of taxation. The UK has led the way in the reform of corporate taxation, demonstrating that it could achieve a much lower average rate of corporation tax than most of its trading competitors by cutting its traditionally high rates. It removed all the special allowances that had accumulated in an effort to offset the very high rates of corporation tax which had begun to limit investment and risk taking. The UK managed to reduce its corporation tax rate from 52 per cent to 35 per cent in a series of manoeuvres which abolished all of the expensive allowances.

But it is the US that has had the courage to extend these principles and to develop them in the sphere of income taxation. As a result, the highest rate of income tax in the US is now 27 per cent, not far off the lowest rate in the UK. There has been a massive simplification and many of the special allowances have been cut out, enabling the yield to be maintained whilst cutting the rates. In all the reforms so far attempted, it has been discovered that a reduction in the total burden and in the high marginal rates has a beneficial effect upon the amount of tax collected. Fewer people think it worth emigrating when the rates are brought down and more people think it worthwhile making a declaration or making a full return of their income. Tax reform, giving back incentive to people to work hard and to set up their own business, is an inseparable part of the story of rebuilding enterprise.

It is this set of ideas which could be called popular capitalism. Popular capitalism is much broader than the simple expansion of ownership by attractive share sales. That is important, for the spread of wider property ownership lies at the core of creating a responsible capitalist society where everyone has a stake in success. But popular capitalism has to be much more. There are many ways of encouraging people to obtain a stake in the commercial life of the country. Fostering small business is a most obvious one and cutting taxes is a good way of fostering small business. Opening up areas of activity that were before the prerogative of the state enables many more businesses to be formed and allows more participants to come into those sectors as principals. Replacing debt with equity may salvage business opportunity and, in its turn, enable ownership to be broadened. The growth of stock markets is an essential prerequisite to the whole process of widening ownership. If people are going to buy, they need a mechanism for selling. They cannot always rely on dealing direct with the government, as they do when purchasing privatisation issues.

This is a coherent world view. The ideas interlock. They address the core of the financial problem of the age, the over-indebtedness of governments and companies in many parts of the world. They also address the core of the social problem of the age. Ever-growing state intervention has created that very kind of alienation that Marx thought he saw in capitalism. The re-introduction of incentive, opportunity and self-enterprise is rebuilding the self-respect, as well as the economic strength of those countries that are trying it. This coherent set of ideas is linked to liberty and is the economic expression of democracy in all its manifestations. These ideas are the most powerful set the world has seen since state-based, nationalisation-based, go-for-planned growth strategies developed in the post-war consensus.

In exactly the same way that the post-war, Marxist-tinged, socialist-dominated consensus of the liberal West went round the world and was tried by many countries, so will this new consensus. And in exactly the same way that those ideas of state intervention, control and ownership were adopted by parties of the right as well as of the left, on this occasion the ideals of popular capitalism will also be adopted by parties on the left as well as on the right. We have already seen in outline how countries of diverse styles and political situations are being attracted to these ideals, for they like the success that they can bring. The history of modern political success and failure is inextricably linked to the attitude parties take to this powerful set of ideas. What seems to matter is the speed at which these ideas are adopted and adapted to local circumstances in each particular country. For, at the core of these ideas lies an understanding that countries are too heavily indebted, and an understanding that in a time of very rapid social, technical and economic change, placing the accent on freer more liberal systems is going to help rather than hinder a country in adjusting to the new spirit of the age.

This thesis will prove contentious to many social democrats and socialists. They will argue that these ideals remain ideological. They will seek to demonstrate that the ideas are partial as an answer to the world's problems. Many of them, particularly in the UK, will continue to argue that only more state money, state direction and nationalisation can possibly provide a solution to endemic economic disorders, but they will be wrong. It is vital to explain what is going on in the political process as it unfolds in many countries.

Let us take the case of the Prime Minister of Australia. Hawke has been re-elected on two separate occasions. He is the first Labour Premier of the Federation of Australia to pull off this singular coup. It is true that his latest victory was in part aided by the split in the opposition party through the crisis engineered by the ambitious Sir Joh, the Premier of Queensland. Without this split in the opposition Hawke may have found it more difficult. But it is also true that opposition parties usually only start to split apart when they sense an underlying failure in their ideas and their response to the situation. For what was happening to the Australian opposition parties was that they were split apart in their response to the powerful ideas of economic liberalism and privatisation. They had to watch, almost helplessly, as Hawke carried out the miracle of moving his party towards accepting a degree of deregulation, and even of private capital and privatisation, that the Conservative opposition would not have accepted 15 years ago. Hawke's third victory is in some ways more remarkable than Margaret Thatcher's victory in the UK, for it took place against a background of bad news on unemployment and with an economy which was far from flourishing. None the less Hawke skilfully exploited some of the new ideas and the weaknesses in the opposition which they had helped to generate, in order to get through to his third remarkable victory.

In New Zealand something similar has begun to happen. The Labour Party under Lange had a hectic first period of administration. Lange and his Finance Minister, Roger Douglas, started to carry out a most extraordinary deregulatory liberalising experiment on the New Zealand economy. Their beliefs and their practice went rather further in liberalising and in making profits the goal of state enterprise than Margaret Thatcher had done in the UK in her early days. Lange, and more especially Douglas, were determined to restore market disciplines to large sectors of the economy which had fallen under state control. For example, Douglas was quite happy to lead a crusade to sack half the coal miners from the state run mines in order to make the mines profitable. His explanation for his action was based entirely upon the need to be commercial and the need to generate money. The social considerations were relegated well to the bottom of the debate. He gave birth to Rogernomics, the third variant of the new economics after Reaganomics in the USA and Thatcherism in the UK.

Lange and Douglas have also been fortunate in their opposition. The conservative National Party opposition in New Zealand has been split right down the middle over how to respond to the liberalising, enterprise-seeking Labour Party that they oppose. One group have wished to move to the right of Lange and Douglas, and to come out fighting for even more rapid deregulation and privatisation. Another group, who have remained the voice of the dispossessed rural poor and of the more backward rural communities in general, feel that Lange and Douglas are leaving behind the poorer agricultural rural areas as their rip-roaring economic deregulation powers a phenomenal economic improvement in the cities but allows the rural areas to languish.

One of the most universal, and perhaps the only damaging charge against the new economics, lies in the alleged divisions it creates. Wherever it has been tried it is discovered that deregulation and freedom stimulates an extremely patchy recovery. Some sectors of the economy and some areas of a country boom very rapidly, whilst others fail to respond quickly or at all. The contrasts become more marked as a result of the phenomenal success that it unleashes in the best sectors and areas. This becomes a natural prey to the politics of jealousy, with those politicians who speak for the areas that are not showing the spirit of enterprise and responding as rapidly as they might, casting doubts on total achievement and drawing attention to the sharp discrepancies and inequalities. They look back nostalgically to an era which was comfortable in the knowledge that greater equality could be pursued through state direction without noticing that the economy was getting out of date or shabby.

Lange's second victory was comfortable. Unemployment was rising. The national opposition party made the most of the alleged divisions in the country and spoke well for the rural areas that seemed disadvantaged. But the enterprise and enthusiasm unleashed in the city was sufficient to carry Lange through and the splits in the opposition, as it wrestled with its soul and with the power of the new ideas, communicated itself to the electorate. We can look forward to a period of division and strife within the National Party of New Zealand as those in favour of a more vigorous understanding and enthusiasm for the new ideas fight for the ascendency and may well attain it.

In Portugal it has also been a left of centre party that has done most to embrace the new ideas. Suarez's great victory, where he confounded the critics and showed that even in the Portuguese system an overall majority of seats can be won, demonstrated once again that a party of the left which was in tune with modern ideas could carry its country. Immediately after election Suarez announced a large-scale programme of privatisation and economic deregulation. He is quite confident that he has 'socialised' this process and has made it Portuguese in its nature. None the less, it bears a remarkable resemblance to privatisation and liberalisation programmes elsewhere.

In both Finland and in Austria a long tradition of left of centre dominance of the parliamentary process has been broken in recent elections. The Finnish and the Austrian Conservatives have both spoken cautiously of the need to privatise and to introduce more private sector disciplines and enterprise into the economy. Their reward has been a major share in power for the first time in many a long year, and a gradual cautious movement towards setting forth policies of private capital for state enterprises.

In France it is impossible to say how well the right will fare. Here the origins of the privatisation and liberalisation process were simply ideological. Born of the bitter struggle against President Mitterand and his 1981 wave of nationalisations, the opposition managed to exploit all the weaknesses of his regime and got its chance to privatise and liberalise. Time will tell how powerful a cocktail this proves in France, but the international evidence is encouraging.

In the Philippines President Aquino rapidly linked her championing of liberty to a programme of strong economic reform. Cory Aquino is one of nature's natural politicians. She has a good sense of what her public require and she is not particularly ideological, other than in her strident and strong belief in freedom and the spirit of Philippines democracy. None the less, she and her advisers have seen the connections between economic liberalisation, debt repayment, privatisations and the kind of economic reforms they wish to see to underpin their new democracy.

When asked to name her philosophy, Aquino says that her position is that of a Christian socialist. She is certainly a Christian first and foremost, but socialism is there in the sense that she does have an intuitive understanding of the needs of the poor Philippinos, and places land reform very high up her list of priorities. Being a realist, she sees that in order to pay for the land reform she needs a pot of money which the Philippine state does not possess. Even if she succeeds in repatriating large fortunes stacked away overseas by

President Marcos during his happy years, she will still need access to much larger sums of money to finance the operation. She comes of a large land-owning family herself and has shown her sacrifice to the cause of the Philippines by staking out the territory. She has made it clear that no family will be above the law and that all large estates have to be subject to land reform with some of their land being redistributed to the poor peasants. She wishes, however, to do this by giving compensation to the existing owners, and that is where the need for extra cash comes in. As a result she has stated that she will use proceeds from a large-scale privatisation programme to pay for the land reform.

Privatisation will not be that easy in the Philippines because many of the state enterprises are bust or virtually worthless because of the way they have been managed in the past, and because of the very large debt burden they have built up. Coupled with the debt-swap programme and new investment, if Aquino succeeds in stabilising the situation to encourage new investors, the thing could work quite well. She is a realist in adapting the new ideas to her own very special brand of Philippino Catholic politics.

In Canada, the political tussle has proved much closer. Both the Liberal and the Conservative parties have expressed interest in the new ideas. Neither side has gained an overwhelming advantage and both sides have been cautious in their adoption or implementation. In Quebec the Liberals have shown the strongest hand. In control of the administration, they have announced a large-scale privatisation programme and are gradually getting it into place. It will fall short of tackling the largest of all the state enterprises, Hydro-Quebec, but it could be far-reaching. At the federal level, where the Conservatives are in control, they have announced a great interest in privatisation but have shown themselves inept and slow to implement the policy. Selling Canada's leading aerospace manufacturer to its American quasi-monopoly rival Boeing was one of the most politically insensitive acts in any privatisation programme worldwide. It set the programme back quite considerably, enabling critics to point out the obvious shortfalls of selling to an overseas competitor, particularly an overseas competitor in a country where there are quite tense trade relations because of the relative size and importance of that country in relation to Canada itself.

It is difficult to predict which way things will move in Canada. It is still possible for the Liberals to outflank the Conservatives at the national level, building on the experiences they are having in Quebec. It would also be possible for the Conservative government in Canada to decide to take the policy more seriously and to get on with the privatisation of Air Canada, Canadian National Railways and so forth. Time will tell. At the moment the Canadian Conservative administration looks rather wobbly and lacks resolve.

It is in the UK that the political analyst must, on this occasion, pause for further contemplation. Whereas in the story of restoring democracy the UK has little to tell us because it created a democracy so many years ago, in the story of privatisation and economic liberalism the UK must be in the forefront. It has had the longest and the largest programme of any country in the world. It had some of the most intractable problems of any advanced country when Margaret Thatcher's administration set out to turn the tide in 1979. And it too has seen a remarkable political phenomenon as a result. Three election victories in a row by Margaret Thatcher's Conservatives is an achievement that no party in power has surpassed for over 170 years in the UK. This is to say nothing of the fact that she is the first ever woman Prime Minister in the UK or in any major Western European country, and leaves aside the fact that she leads a party which, 30 years ago, was traditionally led and represented by people who came from wealthy and privileged backgrounds. She herself has worked her way up from below.

The important thing in the achievement of Margaret Thatcher is that she could persuade the hesitant and heavily socialised British people in 1979, 1983 and 1987 that the new ideas that the Conservative administration had grappled with and adopted represented real hope for the recovery of the country. In the first period of Margaret Thatcher's administration she was extremely timid about privatisation and about wider ownership. Keen on wider home ownership she pursued that with a vengeance. But the bulk of the first period of administration was taken up with tackling the severe union problems facing the country, and with curbing inflation. It was her resolve in achieving that, and beginning a modest economic recovery before the 1983 election, that won her her second term in office. The Falklands saga had a favourable impact but was not the decisive influence as the government's rating in the polls had already started to climb before the Argentinian war.

It was in the second period of government that the administration turned to a serious large-scale privatisation programme and, on the back of that, developed wider ownership from being simply more home ownership to widening share ownership in industry and commerce as well. The results have been quite startling. A new generation of shareholders has quickly developed. The political debate has turned from the question of trade unions, industrial and economic performance to inequalities in the public services. The new question is why the public services now lag so badly behind in public esteem and service quality compared with the private sector industrial and commercial activities.

Equally important to the story of the gradual growth and success of the Thatcher administration are the problems it has produced for the opposition parties. From 1979 onwards the Labour and Liberal parties decided to oppose all of the measures of economic liberalisation and especially privatisation. Both parties argued from the premise that all state intervention in the economy was likely to be good and that only state intervention could protect individuals from profit-seeking capitalists who would have no interest in customer or public service and every interest in exploitation. This simple-minded attitude led to a series of rearguard actions. They opposed bus and coach deregulation, only to see fares decline and services improve. They opposed the sales of Amersham, Cable and Wireless, British National Oil Corporation, National Freight and a host of other public sector companies, only to see their profits and investments soar and their efficiency and performance improve after sale.

By the 1983 election the Labour Party and the Liberals were convinced that they had to dig in in their opposition to these measures. During that election the Labour Party, in conjunction with the Trade Union movement, tried to make a major issue out of the forthcoming privatisation of British Telecom. They argued that the public could be damaged by its privatisation and only by retaining it as a public sector monopoly could the customers' and the employees' interests be protected. They did not succeed in turning it into a major election issue but, in campaigning on it they did discover that the public was not entirely with them. The public was well aware of the shortcomings of British Telecom's service as a public monopoly. Its prices had risen in real terms, although the technology it was using was improving so rapidly that a real price cut should have been possible. The public telephone boxes were often in disrepair or the coins so jammed into the slot that you could not use them. The aging system often delivered people crossed lines or imperfect connections and British Telecom had failed to invest in new lines and new switching.

After the 1983 election defeat, the Labour and Liberal parties continued with their hostility to all privatisation measures. They held the traditional image of capitalism: portly men in pin stripes deciding peoples' futures over wine and cigars. Although the privatisation programme was stepped up, with a tenfold increase in the money value of sales between 1983 and 1986, the opposition became less and less effective. The change in privatisation which caused most difficulties to the Labour and Liberal opposition was the pursuit of wider ownership. After 1983 privatisation became a mass ownership movement, and the political opposition parties began to ask themselves whether it was wise to campaign so heavily against something which was attractive to millions of people. However, as before 1983, so before the 1987 election the Labour Party still promised to renationalise portions of the public estate privatised by the Conservatives. They now threatened not only the gentlemen in the pin stripes but the voter in the bus queue.

At the time of the 1983 election the opposition parties made it clear that they would try and reverse virtually all the denationalisations. In 1987, the Labour Party's policy was less clear. They said they would wish to bring British Telecom and British Gas back under public control and they put forward various half-thought-out schemes that might achieve this without having to spend all the money necessary to renationalise them on the one hand, or without stealing the assets back on the other. The public was not persuaded.

The splinter group, the Social Democrats, who fell out with the Labour Party in 1981 and campaigned as a separate party in both the 1983 and the 1987 elections, were always less clear in their hostility. In 1987, in an alliance with the Liberal Party, they were dragged more towards opposing privatisation. But on the whole over the six year period, the Social Democrats held the view that they themselves would not have privatised anything, but they would not seek to reverse any privatisations the Government had undertaken. Their leader, David Owen, usually out of sympathy with the rank and file of much of his party, was prepared to agree that the liberalisation measures, as opposed to the privatisation measures, had some merit for customer service.

After the 1987 election more drastic rethinking was clearly necessary. As this book is written, it is becoming clear to Labour and even to some Liberal leaders that parts of the economic liberalisation programme are attractive policies and do have something to contribute to economic prosperity and the improvement of customer service. There are a few in the opposition parties now who are even toying with the idea of arguing for much stronger liberalisation moves to break up monopolies and to introduce competitors to public utility services. Were they to do this, the Conservatives would find it much less easy to defend their economic position. There are also those within the opposition parties who see that wider ownership has proved to be a winner. Labour and Liberals must have bitter memories of their futile opposition to the sale of council houses to their tenants. For years these opposition politicians tried to stop people buying their own council houses in their local authority areas. The policy proved overwhelmingly successful and eventually forced a rethink on both Labour and Liberal politicians. The same appears to be happening with their implacable hatred towards the sale of shares. The Liberals have long accepted the principle of employee shareholding. They therefore find it difficult to oppose any sale of assets by the Government if employees and managers are primarily involved as purchasers.

The experience of the British opposition parties should act as a warning to politicians everywhere, whether of the right or of the left. It shows that there has been no joy in opposing liberalisation measures, and little joy in opposing privatisation ones. The only success the opposition parties have had is in exposing service deficiencies in privatised utility monopolies, where the inference must be that the government should have deregulated and liberalised the service rather more. No-one believes that had they remained public monopolies they would have been any better.

There are still those in English political life who look backwards to a new flowering of glorious yesterdays. Many of the Social Democrats, excluding their former leader David Owen, are firmly in this camp. They believe that a little bit more Government intervention, a little more subsidy, a little more egalitarian justice dispensed by well-meaning bureaucrats and politicians from the centre would put right the wrongs they see in the market place. These are the people who believe that opera seats for the well-heeled ought to be subsidised in the interests of culture, who believe that university professors ought to be paid a lot of money without stipulating what they should do for it and who believe that if only the Government got back into the serious business of meddling with industry, the British industrial base could be much larger. Yet these were the self-same people who, in government in 1964–70, and 1974–79, presided over frequent and recurrent economic crises, rising unemployment and a constant slipping of Britain compared with many of its major trading competitors.

The Liberals and Social Democrats attempted to come together in a new 'exciting politics of coalition and consensus'. This was rejected decisively in two elections. Following the 1987 election the public witnessed the spectacle of the coalition brothers who believed in consensus tearing each other apart within 72 hours of the close of the elections. The cynical prospectus of 1987 had been revealed to the public as false by the obvious dislike of the two leading personalities, the liberal leader and the Social Democrat leader, for each other and for each other's views. The modern Liberal Party in the UK is anything but liberal. It has been a traitor to its past and it has evolved into a party which believes in a lukewarm socialist philosophy and sees a state answer to every problem. It is curious that the Liberal Party, a party with a strong tradition of belief in markets and liberal economics, should have torn all that up. It is even stranger that the party which used to sell itself on the basis that it was the party with the exciting new ideas should have been so blind to the opportunities that lie in the new economic thinking. The politics of a little bit more of that and a little bit less of this, the politics of dangerous equipoise between two radically conflicting views of the world and systems is not a politics which has any attraction at the moment. When allied to party members and MPs who seek solace in some Marxist precepts, it is even less alluring. In the UK and in many other countries of the world the public is at last seeing the clarity of the choice. If something is not done to halt the rapid rise of the state and the growth of more and more state power, a free people can be delivered into serfdom by the back door.

So what can the new economics and the new politics deliver? The first hope which is being turned into reality is the chance of faster economic growth. The politics of the 1960s were about the pursuit of growth. In the 1970s, when growth became much more difficult to achieve and the economies of the world were buffeted by oil crisis and recession, some politicians tried to pretend that there were things higher than material values which the public should pursue as an alternative goal. The public was not readily persuaded and the 1980s have seen the rekindling of the hope of greater prosperity in those countries which have lost the knack of growth. The UK economy since 1981 has been a shining example. Following a deep two-year recession, deeper than some other parts of the world although it was an international phenomenon, the UK economy has grown consistently at around 3 per cent per annum ever since. It has been the longest and best sustained period of growth for the economy since World War II. The process of growth has been hastened by the economic liberalisation measures. In a world where technology is changing so dramatically patterns of work and of service and goods provision are also shifting rapidly. This requires relatively free labour markets and flexibility to innovate and change. Successful economies are discovering or rediscovering that the best way of achieving the flexibility the new technology requires is to have a large base of small businesses, to have an entrepreneurial culture in which people can set up new activities fairly readily, and to make sure that the labour market works sufficiently well so that skills can be reapplied, new skills learned and people transferred rapidly.

Next, the new economics can deliver both lower prices and better services. The powerful truth that competition is the only true guardian of the customer interest is being re-established. As the great monopolies are loosened or removed, prices nearly always fall and there is usually a rapid increase in the range and the quality of services provided. Take, for example, the decision in several countries to remove the monopoly that the public telephone system had over the provision of user equipment to add on to the network. In each of the cases where this has happened — the US, the UK, France and now New Zealand — there has been a sharp increase in the style and range of equipment that can be provided and a fall in its price. This is not accidental. As new providers come into the market and get a direct contact with the customer they have to offer something extra in order to win a market share. In its turn the old public monopoly has to respond by trying to improve its performance. The net result is nearly always a much expanded market, a lower market share for the former monopolist and a better deal for the customer.

The new economics brings with it a greater mobility, which as we have seen, is both its strength and, some would say, its weakness. It gets many out of the equality of misery which the socialist and neo-Marxist state provides, but as the contrasts become greater between the poor who are no worse off and the better off who are better off, so the opposition to the inequalities become shriller. In the UK, the dispossessed are heavily concentrated in the centres of the old industrial cities. It is this problem which enterprise capitalism and the economics of the market place now has to tackle with vigour. There are those who claim that the existence of inner-city problems in the UK is evidence that the marketplace will always be unfair and will leave sink areas where there is no hope. It is possible to reply that many of the problems of the British cities have been created by government and local authority intervention. The characteristics of the deprived inner-cities in the UK are: a very high proportion of municipal house ownership: a very high level of taxation which drives business away: a complete unattractiveness to new enterprise or to enterprising people, who find it easier and better to move out to the suburbs or the rural areas to locate their new businesses and build their new homes. This problem is now being tackled as the government tries to override municipal socialism, recycling the land and redeveloping the cities in a way that is sympathetic to the new spirit of business activity. New Zealand is going to have to find a similar answer to the problem of rural deprivation which labour government policies are highlighting.

There are some who claim that another direct result of the new economics is unemployment. They point to the substantial rise in unemployment under the Conservative government in the UK. They point to the sharp increase in unemployment in New Zealand under Lange's deregulating Labour government. But the evidence is not as unequivocal as they claim. Unemployment was rising in most countries of the world in the early 1980s when the UK saw its sharpest increase in unemployment. In socialist France, for example, the rise was also marked and was one of the many factors that led to a reversal of policy in favour of a more deregulatory privatisation-based policy. In the US and in Japan the economies were much more successful in keeping unemployment down or in reducing it once it had risen in the recession. The enormous versatility of those economies seemed to be based upon a very widespread small business culture, on much greater mobility of entrepreneurial activity and much less state control and intervention in the dynamics of change.

The fact that unemployment has been falling rapidly in the UK for more than a year gives some cause for encouragement. There is no necessary correlation between the new economics of deregulation and rising unemployment. Indeed there is every reason to suppose that the deregulatory measures have been beneficial for jobs. It stands to reason that if costs and prices are lowered, if service quality improves and if the volume of business expands there is likely to be more employment than if business is on the defensive, subject to the depredations of foreign competition. There is no doubt that the New Zealand and the UK policies of sorting out public enterprises prior to privatisation, or just for the sake of improving their efficiency, was a necessary step which did, in the

short run, increase unemployment. There were massive redundancies from the state sector in the UK and there are now large
redundancies from the state sector in New Zealand. In the case of
the UK this did not represent a marked shift of policy, as there
had been huge job losses in the coal, steel and shipbuilding industries
throughout the post-war period under administrations of all political
persuasions. None the less, at a time of world recession the imposi-
tion of large redunancies in the public enterprises in a desperate
effort to make them more efficient was a contributory factor to the
rising unemployment.

To sum up, the new economics offers the hope of breaking out
of drab utilitarian greyness. It is a process which entails breaking
out at varying speeds in different countries, at different times in
different parts of the same countries and in different industries. It
takes time to rebuild an entrepreneurial culture where one has been
lost. It takes time for a public to adjust to the idea that making
money is not necessarily an evil thing and that the process of
economic change requires the accumulation of capital by individuals
and families.

Popular capitalism is in its essence the democracy of the
marketplace. It tackles directly the alienation from the state and
the bureaucracy which have been felt worldwide as the state has
grown. A free market can provide redress through recourse to the
law or simply a change of supplier. In a bureaucratic system allocation is everything and the only redress is through the political
process. Bureaucracies and state run societies become hierarchical.
People are ranked according to their position in the bureaucratic
or political hierarchy and they are favoured according to the
contribution they make to the ruling party. Popular capitalism is,
in contrast, anarchic and democratic in its style. It does not matter
who you are, who your parents were, where you came from: it is
who *you* are and what you can contribute that matters. All popular
capitalist societies have absorbed the message of welfare economics
of the mid-twentieth century. All democratic politicians building
a policy of popular capitalism believe that some of the wealth
generated by the process should be collected in taxes and used to
look after the poor, the ill and the weak. But those same politicians
also believe it is vitally important that the stage is never reached
where practically everyone is categorised as disadvantaged or poor
or weak or ill so that there is no-one left generating the wealth to
support the better tomorrow.

Are we witnessing the death of Marxism and the death of

socialism? I think it is unlikely that anything so dramatic can happen. But I do believe that we are witnessing a substantial shift in world opinion. The world will never be as naive again as it was in the early twentieth century in its appraisal of socialist and Marxist claims about the perfections of the socialist society and the joys of unrestricted egalitarianism. Many now understand that Marxism easily becomes corrupted, that the state does not wither away, and that freedoms can rapidly be eroded or destroyed.

As we witness this fascinating struggle between popular enterprise capitalism on the one hand and the older creeds of socialism and Marxism on the other, social democracy itself is getting squeezed. People now have to sign up and make a choice. And what is happening in many parts of the world is that people are now, for the first time, coming down on the side of freedom and popular enterprise. Well might they do so, given the power of that system to deliver and the examples around the world where it has delivered. It is the alert political party which backs this movement, whether it was originally a party for the right or left. And given the emphasis in popular capitalism on the spread of wealth and ownership and the participation of employees in ownership, as well as in the wealth-creating process, it is a hybrid creed which is neither clearly of the right or of the left. It is simply the most powerful political idea on offer to this generation.

3

The Road to Ruin: The World in Hock to Bankers

Of oil and Eurobonds

There was borrowing, borrowing everywhere but a marked reluctance to lend. The oil crisis in 1973 brought to prominence a growing problem in the international financial world. In 1973 when the Arabs discovered that they could put up the price of oil substantially and still hope to sell a reasonable quantity of their staple commodity they triggered a series of massive transfers of money around the world through a financial system that had to adjust rapidly if it was to survive. The 1960s and early 1970s had been years of growth. The growth had fuelled and had been fuelled by a major expansion in international credit as banks participated in the growth and offered money to companies and individuals prepared to expand and invest.

The sudden huge transfer of income from the Western industrial countries to the oil-producing states jolted the system. More importantly the undeveloped Third World, which did not have oil, had to pay large amounts in hard currencies to the oil-producing states. This changed the patterns of international finance dramatically for a decade. Whilst wise men pondered and committees met, the banking system quietly got on with the task of taking the flows of monies to the Middle East and routing them back to the developing and more especially to the developed world. The euro finance markets became important intermediaries. The world paid for its oil in dollars. The Arabs lodged their dollars in the US banking system. The US banks took the dollars offshore and lent them to companies and governments worldwide.

The Arab states played their part in the adjustment process. Within a few years of the major increase in the oil price many of them had discovered ways of spending the money, largely by purchasing investment and consumption goods from the Western industrial world. This recycled the cash and reduced strains on their balance of payments. Those states that maintained a large balance of payment surplus, like Saudi Arabia, soon discovered that they needed to invest their monies through the world's financial markets. It was Saudi money which lay behind the expansion of the American and European banking systems in the early explosive growth of the euro markets in the mid-1970s. Saudi money found its way to London and New York for investment in portfolios of claims on the Western industrialised world. From cautious deposits and short-term bonds it circulated into the Western banking and money market systems. Gradually Arab money found its way into some longer-term and riskier investments. Without these twin adjustments to the strains of the oil price shock the world economy would have suffered badly.

By 1979 some semblance of order had returned. The Western countries had adjusted to the new patterns of demand and the Western financial markets had adjusted to the new sources of short-term and long-term capital. The main sufferers, as so often, were the developing countries with no oil reserves of their own. Discussions about the possibility of forming cartels to bolster the prices of tin, cocoa, coffee or other staple commodities floundered in the different market circumstances they faced. There was to be no easy solution to the problems of the impoverished Third World unless they themselves found oil. Only in this commodity did the supply/demand balance favour high prices and income beyond the dreams of avarice.

The second oil shock was in some ways a crueller blow. The chance events of Iranian politics and the sharp contraction in Iranian supplies of oil to the international market lay behind the second great surge in the price of oil taking it up to $30 a barrel, where some ten years before it had been a mere $2. In 1974 the Western industrial world first tried to get used to the idea of using less oil and then decided it was easier to export more in order to pay for the oil. Now, in 1980, they needed to do the same again. The Japanese, who had been quicker off the mark in 1974 in seeing the significance of reducing the oil-dependence of their economy as rapidly as possible, were once again the swiftest to respond to the surge in the price. Their ambitious programme of reducing oil-use soon made an impact. For the first time, Western Europe and, to a lesser extent, the United States, began to take seriously the idea of making do with less. A wave of energy conservation investment was triggered and the search was on for non-oil-dependent processes and activities. The growing shift of some parts of the old industrial world away from heavy industry to services hastened the process by which the oil-dependence of these economies was reduced.

Meanwhile things were deteriorating at a pace in the developing world. In countries as far apart as the Philippines and Argentina, Jamaica and Brazil, the policy of growth at any price was buoyed up by massive expansion of credit from US banks to the governments and companies within those countries. It became a sign of virility in the US financial markets to put more loans on your books. Throughout the late 1970s and into the early 1980s there was a feeling that country risk was no real risk at all. People went through the motions of hiring credit analysts and even political analysts to write learned papers about the ability of different countries to service their debts. But in the late 1970s it was the salesman who was in the ascendancy and what mattered was writing more business. Business was available in impecunious Third World countries and so it was to impecunious Third World countries that senior bankers took their first class air flights.

There were times when analysts compounded the difficulties that the loan salesmen were creating. In the early 1980s one of the best credit risks of all was thought to be Mexico, for here was the Third World country in great need of development finance which had its own access to oil and oil revenues. What could possibly go wrong as all the investments being made and the money being advanced could be underwritten by the high price of oil?

Exporting Herbert Morrison's dream

In the 1950s and 1960s one of the tablets of stone, the received wisdom, of development economics was that government-to-government lending, coupled with aid monies and the growth of state enterprises in developing countries, could provide the panacea for all the ills the developing country faced. In the name of faster growth more and more aid money was pushed in to the poorest countries. In the name of faster growth more money was lent government-to-government particularly to sponsor large projects on a grandiose scale.

Most especially the tablets of stone had inscribed on them Britain's leading intellectual export of the 1950s: the concept of the Morrisonian public corporation. Here was to be the answer to all the difficulties of getting things done in Third World countries. Where markets might seize up, where people might be unwilling, where governments might be corrupt or subject to *coups* and changes in political fortune, the miraculous Morrisonian corporation would go on forever with that same sense of public purpose and grand moral vision which its original founder in the UK had embodied firmly in it. People asked too little about whether the Morrisonian corporation might take root in alien cultures in quite the same way. Nor did any consider the possibility that the Morrisonian corporation was itself doing great damage to the UK economy — not renowned for its fine performance in the 1950s and 1960s. UK residents went about their business of exporting their ideas unperturbed.

One of the most remarkable intellectual exports of all time was the nationalised industry corporation. It had immediate appeal to the recipient countries. Here was a corporation which was not theoretically under direct government control. Yet it received its board appointments from the government, it could be influenced by the government in a whole variety of covert and explicit means, it could provide a monopoly so that the government could gain a stranglehold over crucial sectors of the economy, and it provided a reputable conduit for foreign aid and foreign lending. The overseas bankers liked it because they liked the implicit guarantee of its revenues and capital by the state which sponsored it. Domestic politicians liked it because they could manipulate it, often seeing it as the quickest route to pork barrel politics. And those given the honorific task of running the public corporations liked it too, when it often represented an easy route to fame and recognition without the dire necessity to face competitors in the marketplace which so many private businesses faced.

Travelling the world today the evidence of this enormous intellectual activity is there for everyone to see. Across the face of the globe there are public corporations in various states of preparedness, in varying degrees of debt, beset by poor quality service, bureaucratic administration and difficult relations with their sponsor governments and Third World agencies. The transport sector was everywhere thought to be a suitable case for treatment. Railways around the world were built as centralised national systems, immediately incorporated as public corporations. There are few private railways left, although there are some in the United States, one in Canada and a number of private lines eking out a precarious living on the edge of nationalised networks elsewhere. Buses around the world, scarcely an industry requiring great central direction and huge capital investment, were also heavily nationalised. Governments came to believe that only they could work out what routes needed running and only they could protect the interests of the travelling public. Public utilities were caught up in the enthusiasm for state solutions. There are few electricity, water, gas or telephone systems around the world that are not under state control. And as the movement went on, a great variety of industrial and agricultural processes got carried up in the nationalisation fervour, including, throughout the Third World, the national organisation of the marketing of a variety of staple agricultural products.

The growth of state enterprise and of government involvement in the process of regeneration and growth compounded the difficulties as the 1960s and 1970s wore on. High budget deficits became unsustainable. Large industrial complexes under government control or guidance needed ever larger sums of money to pay the losses as well as to meet the capital costs. Public spending mounted as restless people understandably demanded welfare programmes before the countries had the wherewithal to pay for them. The coming of television and jet travel for the masses brought to people's eyes images of luxury and wealth that they would never have seen before. The impact was explosive on the politics of developing countries.

Growth and recycling

There were those who saw the answer in the dash for growth through the expansion of deficits of all kinds. Why not borrow more money for growth? Why not borrow more money to tide the country over a temporary embarrassment whilst the export earnings built up — if they ever did? Others felt the answer lay in yet more aid and more ambitious intervention in the economies of the developing world by the developed world. US administrations spawned huge departments under the control of the State Department full of experts able to travel anywhere at a moment's notice to offer yet more advice, help and solace to those countries going through these periods of 'temporary difficulties' or 'structural imbalance'. The politicians of the developing world came to see their ambit as lying somewhere between the State Department, the World Bank, the International Monetary Fund and the other large international conferences. The great conference-going circuit developed, with the senior politicians and senior officials of the Third World countries mixing easily in the smart hotels and the luxurious limousines that were routine for those coming to advise them from the developed world. Old world met new, poor world met rich on the terms of the rich new world. The large multinational organisations set up after the War to build a new world were in their element, hob-nobbing with Prime Ministers and Finance Ministers. The post-war settlement did not percolate very far down in many of the poor and developing countries, although its made its impact on the life-style of international advisers, politicians and senior officials in all countries.

The 1970s and 1980s were also characterised by fast technological growth. The pace of change accelerated with the coming of the micro-chip making possible a new form of robotics which revolutionised the production processes of the developed world. A new dimension was added by information technology as the large lumbering punch card machines of the 1960s became the small sophisticated highly powerful electronic gadgets of the 1980s. The total computing power in the hands of a large company in the developed world in the early 1960s could be provided in a modest package, on a single desk, at very little cost, in any part of the world by the late 1980s.

This changing technology brought havoc to many older parts of the world's industrial structure and made the task of regeneration and growth in the Third World in some ways yet more complicated. The level of skills required to produce the new industries and operate the new processes was much greater than the level of skill required in the old electro-mechanical and mechanical age.

The financial institutions were changing rapidly too. The 1960s and 1970s were characterised by a move away from prudence. The relationship between equity and new debt advances became less and less cautious as the years went on. US banks, often prevented from state hopping by US banking legislation, looked for new ways to develop and make their businesses grow. They found it by developing their corporate and investment banking activities, becoming leading participants in international markets around the world, with a keen interest in the growth of the securities and investment businesses. Computing power and improved international tele-communications made possible an ever faster speed of transfer of data and information across the continents. International security houses developed their skills through the rising eurobond market to encompass lending from one continent to another with systems for assessing risk and measuring return and reward around the world's businesses and countries.

The American banks were amongst the leaders in the euro market boom of the 1970s. Not only was their domestic expansion hindered by the prohibition of inter-state banking, but also their domestic businesses were restrained by Federal reserve requirements. Meanwhile US multinationals were seeking large investment funds throughout the 1960s and early 1970s to build up their businesses within the European marketplace. The US government decision to restrict capital export for direct investment added further stimulus to the growth of the eurobond bonanza. In 1965 eurobanking was almost unknown. By 1980 total bank liabilities amounted to some 1000 billion dollars. The US banks had completed a somersault by reorienting their loan portfolios away from their domestic and towards their overseas businesses. For example, in 1972 Chase Manhattan had an outstanding loan portfolio of $11.27 billion through domestic offices and only $3.7 billion through its overseas offices. By 1981 this had been reversed with the $19.9 billion through domestic offices overtaken by the $27.8 billion through its overseas offices. A similar pattern could be observed at Citi-Corp where, in 1972, the $10.6 billion of lending through domestic offices exceeded the $8.2 billion of the overseas, whereas in 1981 the overseas lending of $41.8 billion exceeded domestic at $30.2 billion.

There was an explosion of euro-lending throughout the late 1970s and early 1980s. New loans amounted to some $20 billion in 1975. In 1981 a staggering total of $148 billion was recorded. Money had been lent on a grand scale to the non-oil developing countries — in 1976 $21 billion; by 1981 $50 billion. Much of this lending had been via a syndicated credit to a para-statal agency or nationalised industry in a developing country backed by a government or central bank guarantee. Much of this process, generated by the US banks in conjunction with their own multinational companies, was quite independent of the oil crisis, although it would be silly to ignore the impact of Middle Eastern monies on the euro markets at the same time. The two reinforced each other in an interesting way.

In the late 1980s a similar process is at work as the Japanese banks travel the world in pursuit of profitable avenues for the investment of their large balance of payment surpluses, and as they try to give support to their expanding multinational industrial base. It is now the Japanese industrial companies which are most likely to make the new investments in the Western industrial world and in the developing world in basic and new electronic industries.

Some people have seen in this period of financial instability, this period of creaking banking institutions and rapid technical and economic change, parallels with the difficult period of the late 1920s and early 1930s. During that fateful five years countries reneged on their debts when they found problems too great, many came off the gold standard and tried by the gentle means of depreciation to reduce the burden of external payments debt had placed upon them. More importantly, the main motor of the world economy, the US, found itself in increasing difficulties with a spate of bankruptcies and runs on the banks. The US pursued a violently deflationary strategy and the result was a great recession spreading from the US, with its epicentre on Wall Street and the eastern seaboard.

There are those today who would like to see a similar great deflation as the positive policy response to the inflationary decades of the 1960s and 1970s. The economist Hayek has often argued that only a major deflation can succeed in breaking the vicious inflationary spiral. When asked what this might mean for the state of the world economy and the state of the world banks, he non-chalantly replied that it would mean the bankruptcies of many banks and a massive contraction of credit. So far, through the 1970s and 1980s, a massive contraction of credit on the scale of the early 1930s has been avoided. In consequence the developing world has not been driven into even worse grinding poverty, nor has the plight of the developed world been made that much more difficult.

Yet, in some of the most over-extended Latin American coun-tries the painful medicine of deflating demand and reducing activity in an effort to bring balance of payments into equilibrium, or into surplus, in order to service the debt, has been every bit as stringent as the medicine doled out in the 1930s. The main difference between now and the 1930s has been the much-debated decision by the US to go for growth on the back of twin enormous deficits. The US authorities have been prepared to countenance an ever growing burden of public debt as their budget remains in substantial imbalance, and prepared to run large balance of payments deficits, permitting overseas countries, especially Japan, to build up an ever bigger array of claims on the US economy itself. This decision has in some ways ameliorated and in some ways worsened the problem.

The consequence of the American balance of payments imbal-ance has been the virtual cessation of new lending by American banks to developing countries. No longer does America have capital to spare to ease the growth and development pressures of the developing world. Yet at the same time sustaining the large American market has enabled the virile exporters, particularly the industrial exporters like Japan, to exploit the largest and most prosperous market of the world on a grand scale. It has kept world demand slightly above what it otherwise would have been. It has provided a home for footloose monies in so far as people have thought that the US represents a safe haven in view of its long-standing tradition of political stability, of honouring debts and of the wealth generated in earlier decades.

But the US deficits are also a source of instability. The logic of compound arithmetic is such that within a few years the pace of new spending has to be cut or taxes raised. Within a few years the US balance of payment deficit has to be narrowed and overseas investors will become more reluctant to finance the long-standing American boom. This will strain an even longer-standing American dream. The first signs of this strain became visible in October of 1987 with the crash of many international markets.

The dimensions of the world problem are huge. Heavily indebted nations needing money to develop find it more and more difficult to get money from anybody. American banks, with large portfolios of loans extended to developing countries have become frightened about the risks they have been running, and have to rein back because the American economy no longer has surplus cash to lend overseas. Bankers around the world, having lived through two decades of glorious expansion and become less and less prudent, suddenly gaze out over the precipice into a void and it strikes terror into their hearts. As all banking rests upon confidence, as soon as the lenders themselves begin to fear that they have lent too much credit becomes difficult to get: with its scarcity its price rises. As its price rises, as the rate of interest goes up, so the difficulties of those who have borrowed too much are compounded yet again.

Coupled with this problem are a whole series of underlying difficulties in the process of development itself and in the style of development adopted in many parts of the Third World. The world's development industry had been organised on government-to-government lines. It was back-to-back and shoulder-to-shoulder between government and development agencies around the world. It didn't work very well. Many poor countries kept on borrowing, kept on taking the medicine and the advice, kept on setting up more parastatal organisations but few of them, by this means, broke out of the vicious circle of poverty and deprivation that engulfed them. When this was coupled with a massive change in technology, which even the sophisticated Western nations were hard put to keep up with, and with a volatile price of oil, a basic commodity for most industrial activities, the problems became grave indeed.

It is the purpose of this book to chart some of the troubled waters of the financial crisis and to point to some of the ways through. For there is a passage that can be found without wrecking the world's economy. There is no need to lurch towards the massive deflationary policies advised by some of the severe monetarists, who see in the whole process an almost biblical retribution for the excesses of the past. Nor is there any need on the other hand to lurch with Keynes — doing great dishonour to a great man's name and works — and suggest that a little compassion, care and forgiveness over the exact amount of debt, and some reshuffling of the paper in the parastatal organisations would be enough to see us through. In its origins it is a problem created by an over-expansion of government-to-government credit and private banking credit trading with government guarantees. It is not possible to solve the problem by tampering with the form of that government-to-government capital or by advancing more of it. It is only possible to solve it by embracing the very popular capitalism which is already in the wind.

Debts and capital flight

Many thousands of pages and many millions of words have been expended arguing for different types of debt forgiveness as a solution to the world's debt problems and the crisis of the developing countries. There are those who think that simply extending the term of the debt would be sufficient, as then the countries will only have to meet interest payments and not capital repayments. There are those who believe that the debt has to be rescheduled not only as to its term but also as to its interest rate. They would like to see the Western nations agree to a lower rate of interest on the stock of the debt and at the same time make new advances so that the process of development borrowing can begin all over again.

There are those who believe that if the US cut its budget deficit it could then reduce the real rate of interest in the US through market forces and this in its turn would be enough to cut the rate of interest for the Third World. There is some truth in this proposition, but its advocates must remember there would also be a drop in world demand and that not all of the interest rate decline which might take place would necessarily flow through to those countries whose credit ratings are already poor. There are those who see the solution in new monstrous international organisations. Why not, say some, set up a grand international bank or an extended world bank which could act as banker to all the central banks and could take over some of the international debts and nurse the poorer economies back to health? Either this becomes a more forceful kind of world bank, meting out deflationary medicine to its captive clients as the price for some additional lending, or it becomes a way of retiring the existing debt by granting subsidies to the Third World or reducing the payments charges on the old debt out of some international slush fund. Neither of these methods seems likely to produce the desired results.

It will not be long before all the developing countries realise that it pays to borrow on a huge scale and then to demand some stay of execution. Once the line is broken and too many reschedulings undertaken, which allow forbearance on interest or capital or both, then all the principles on which international lending are based are destroyed. It is no longer worthwhile to be a good borrower meeting the repayments and the interest bills on time. It pays to renege. It would not be difficult to turn the matter into one of international politics and to use the north/south dialogue and the conferences of the poorer nations as vehicles to exploit the situation at the expense of the richer world.

Nor, on the other hand, can there be much joy for the world if the only future that the world's poorest countries have to look forward to is ever greater cuts in living standards as they struggle manfully to pay the interest on debts advanced in the past on a scale far too great given the resources of their feeble economies. Had all that government-to-government lending worked, and had all those projects and parastatals come good, the interest burden on their debt far from becoming unmanageable, would have become easier and easier. One of the principles of development economics through government-to-government loans must be that the rate of productive investment and the improvement in the volume and value of goods exported must exceed the build-up in the interest payments and capital repayments on the debt. This was a simple principle which many bankers had in mind as they calculated their exports/GDP and debt interest/export ratios, which did not seem to have any real bearing upon their decision-making. Alternatively, some bankers decided to rely upon the Western financial institutions and governments who told them it would be alright, who suggested to them that their loans were guaranteed, or who agreed with the banks' rosy forecast of how the investment would work and justify all the money they had advanced.

One of the most noticeable characteristics of the developing world is the problems that the heavily indebted countries have in maintaining capital within their country. Most of the middle range of developing countries, in South America and the Caribbean, have a group of quite wealthy people at their top. But these people often prefer to route their money out of the country for investment in the US or in Switzerland, despite the existence of stringent exchange controls in most of these countries. It might be thought that in a developing country there are far more exciting opportunities for making a good return on capital than in the highly competitive developed world. Certainly there are many goods and services not readily available in the domestic market from domestic sources, some not available at all. There are often many idle hands and there is some spending power in the home population. Yet, despite these natural advantages, the phenomenon of capital flight is still all too common in the developing world.

The response of governments has been to impose more and more stringent controls upon the movement of monies across the exchanges. This has undoubtedly made life more difficult for those who wish to take their money out but not impossible. There are sophisticated methods for earning money abroad or routing money abroad and many rich people in developing countries have numbered bank accounts in Switzerland or anonymous sources of wealth in Miami or New York. There are some excellent stamp and painting collections in various South American countries, natural havens for money people cannot get out of the country immediately; a highly mobile store of value in case of political or financial difficulties.

A recent study by Morgan Guarantee Trust bankers of New York has attempted to quantify the enormous problem of capital flight from the Third World. The capital outflows from countries that needed to import substantial amounts of money to keep themselves going amounted to $250,000 million for the period 1974–85. It was equal to a one-third increase in these countries' external debt over the period. Of these total capital outflows a large proportion could be viewed as capital flight. That is, it was money that could easily have been invested in the domestic economy but which rich individuals and companies deliberately decided to send overseas because they were worried about devaluation, political uncertainty and the health of the domestic economy. The worst affected areas were the heavily indebted countries of Africa and of Latin America.

This has meant that the international banks have become intermediaries between domestic savers and investors in Third World countries. International banks have accepted deposits from rich individuals and companies trying to get their money out of their countries, and have accepted the redenomination of these deposits into hard currencies. They then had to re-lend this and other money to the countries concerned, in the form of state or public sector loans, also often in hard currency. Once the banks started to slow or stop the process of lending new money, the capital exported became an immediate loss of resource in the country concerned.

In order to halt this process, the countries experiencing capital flight have to make their economies more attractive to local investors. This may entail putting up interest rates, as often there are two- or three-tier interest rate structures in these countries, deliberately designed to penalise the domestic investor. It may mean pursuing a more cautious monetary and fiscal policy, so that the currency is more likely to keep its value. It almost certainly entails ending exchange controls. As soon as a country imposes exchange controls people realise that it must be worthwhile getting out. If the government does not have confidence that domestic money will stay in the country to be used in the domestic economy without controls, why should anybody else? It then becomes a worthwhile exercise to find a way over the hurdle.

Table 3.1 shows the scale of the problem and also the way it accelerated in the late 1970s and early 1980s, when the debt problem was also gathering momentum.

The problem of mediating between these great pressures of those trying to get their money out, and governments wishing to attract

Table 3.1: Capital flight from capital-importing countries ($ billion, annual average)

Region	1975–78	1979–82	1983–85	Total
Africa	1.7	4.1	1.8	28.5
Asia	-0.8	7.0	-2.2	18.3
Europe	1.1	2.7	3.0	24.0
Non-oil Middle East	0.2	-0.7	2.7	6.2
Western hemisphere	3.7	14.7	11.0	106.6

Source: IMF, reproduced in *Financial Times*, September 1987

money back into the countries, despite the poor state of the economy, was one of the main reasons why so much strain was placed on the banking system by Third World borrowers. The American banks rapidly tried to change their portfolios when they began to realise that the underlying security in many countries and many companies was not as good as they had anticipated.

None the less, the problem gathered momentum throughout the 1980s. In 1986, for example, 145 American banks failed or were helped to merge. Almost 1500 banks in the US were thought to be in considerable financial difficulty at the end of 1986. In the same year 2 of Canada's big 14 banks failed and Japan's sixth largest bank had to be rescued. All the banks were under considerable pressure on their balance sheets. As they had advanced more and more money to companies and countries unlikely to be able to repay it in full or on time their balance sheets became more and more strained.

Three clear problems emerged. Banks needed much larger reserves against the bad debts in their portfolio. It was no longer realistic in the 1980s to assume that 100 per cent of all the money advanced to Brazil, Mexico or Peru was going to be repaid. Second, the Federal Reserve began to impose different capital ratios in an effort to make the banking system more prudent and cautious. This has placed a further requirement to raise more capital at exactly the same time that the existing capital base was thought to be over-stated by the amount of the loans outstanding that were not going to be repaid. The third factor complicating the position for the American banks has been their wish to expand within the US itself both geographically and by product line as the strict controls preventing banking across state borders and preventing the movement into parallel financial activities have been eroded.

Western banks change their ways

Some of the banks have ballooned their off-balance-sheet commitments in an effort to deal with the problems of their chronic capital inadequacy whilst wishing to continue to expand their businesses. By September 1986 the biggest seven US banks had expanded their off-balance sheet commitments to a staggering $1.4 trillion. This compared with their balance sheet commitments of only $550 billion. In an era when profits are under pressure anyway, this level of off-balance-sheet commitment is worrying.

The system has shown itself to have some resilience during this period of stress. In 1984 the failure of Continental Illinois, the seventh largest bank in the US, was absorbed by the system. In Europe the collapse of Herstatt was also accommodated, although the psychological shock to the system was for a time quite severe.

In an effort to make advances more manageable and more tradable a number of financial innovations have been made. One of the most powerful mechanisms of the late 1970s for advancing money to Third World countries and larger companies was the syndicated bank loan. Banks accepted that individually they could not tolerate the size or degree of risk of an individual loan and so they clubbed together and all had a portion of the syndicated credit. Unfortunately, the credit was not readily tradable and the liquidity of the asset proved to be one of the problems that compounded the balance-sheet difficulties into which the banks sank. In the early 1980s the international bond started to replace the syndicated bank loan. The idea was to raise the money in a form which was readily tradable so that the banks could sell on their interest in the bond issue to third parties who had capital. There have been occasions in the recent past when the bonds have also been fairly illiquid. None the less, the experiments are mushrooming and there is no doubt that banks have to continue innovating and investing in credits that are more tradable, and have to bring more people into the process of advancing money to the Third World by encouraging portfolio investors to take on various kinds of bond instrument.

The gradual erosion of the McFadden rules against interstate banking in the States has had an ironical twist to it. The McFadden rules stopping a bank from one state banking in another were designed following the last period of great financial crisis and tension in the 1930s. The idea behind the proposal was to encourage competition and limit the overstretching of balance sheets. In the 1960s and 1970s banks found a way round the rules by moving into international business; in the 1980s they have done it by the gradual erosion of the rules. Of the 50 states, 39 now allow outsiders to buy into a state bank and this has become a way round the McFadden regulations. Another product of the financial difficulties of the 1930s were the Glass-Steagall rules, preventing a deposit-taking bank also undertaking investment banking. This constraint is also now under re-examination and its applicability is questionable given the need for deposit-taking and lending banks to be able to trade their credits in a securitised form.

The coming of the Japanese

What has been bad news for the US has been good news, by and large, for Japan. The figures demonstrating Japanese enthusiasm to get into syndicated credits and the bond markets raise questions as to whether a major factor in the Third World debt crisis is not simply the difficulties caused by the transfer of the obligation to maintain the flow of cash to these countries from the US to Japan. The Japanese have had to accept a wider range of obligations to a wider range of countries and companies as their enormous trade surpluses have built up. Conversely, the US has had to cut back drastically on its overseas lending as it has become a capital importing country. The magnitude of the switch underway can be illustrated by the eurobond market. As recently as 1984 US banks took over half of the primary eurobond market. It was a market they had founded and dominated for years. In the first quarter of 1987 US banks only took one quarter of all the new issues of eurobonds whereas Japan was up from a modest 9 per cent to almost one third of the total. The market has seen a rapid securitisation as syndicated euro dollar loans have been substituted by tradable bonds. The euro equity and the euro commercial paper markets have also started to grow apace. By 1987 the euro equity market was turning over $1 billion a day, although most of any euro equity issue goes back to the domestic equity market of the company concerned. There will have to be more steps taken to increase the volume of the international equity markets, as so many of the risks that have been assumed by banks and purchasers of bonds are in effect an equity risk and more suitable to equity owners.

In the world today the continuing Japanese surplus guarantees the dominance of Japanese banks and brokers in the US and in Europe. In 1987, Nomura, the giant Japanese house, was at the top of the league table of eurobond underwriters for the first time. Nomura and its fellow Japanese houses can look forward to several years of international dominance. The Japanese began their attack upon the European markets by going for the basic bulk lending to governments and local authorities. They bought themselves a market share by offering more advantageous rates. They used joint ventures and acquisitions of existing US and UK businesses to acquire the skills and the technology they needed. They are now going on from their bulk low-technology entry into the market to deploy an ever wider range of skills and to add more value to their services. By 1987, Japan accounted for 40 per cent of London's foreign currency lending and will soon be the principal market player in eurobonds and syndicated credits.

In the future Nomura, Dai-Ichi and Sumitomo will be dominant banks throughout Europe and the US and their names will be as well known as Sony, Toshiba, Honda and Datsun are now. In the electronics and automobile sectors the names of Sony, Toshiba, Datsun and Honda were little known 30 years ago, or were thought to be greatly inferior to their German and American rivals. Today they have a reputation for quality as well as for world domination. The same could well become true of the Japanese financial houses. The startling fact is that we are well on the road to Japanese domination already. Of the world's 25 largest banks (measured by their assets), 16 are now Japanese. Dai-Ichi is already the world's largest bank overall and Nomura is the dominant securities house. By comparison National Westminster is only the seventh largest bank in the world with eleven Japanese banks larger than Britain's largest. Measured by stock exchange capitalisation — a measure which flatters the Japanese because of the very high price earnings multiples recorded by their stock market — Nomura is an enormous organisation. Salomon Inc., Wall Street's best known securities firm, has a stock market value of just over $5000 million. Nomura has a capitalisation of $66,000 million. That is also eight times larger than the capitalisation of America's largest bank, Citi-Corp.

The Japanese banks take almost two thirds of the US municipal letter of credit business, lending to local authorities, and take some 40 per cent of the British local authority bond market. There are now 70 Japanese security houses in the City of London alone. The Japanese are at last building up an appetite for foreign equity. In 1986 they purchased foreign equity worth over $20,000 million. They need to go on buying more and more if the world balance between debt and equity is to improve. For it is Japanese fire power which will be the main determinant of the speed of the re-capitalisation of bankrupt companies and countries worldwide. (*Sunday Telegraph* 23 August 1987).

Counting the cost of lending

What impact has all this had on individual banks? The depredations caused by bad lending have been massive. In 1987 a brave decision was made by Citi-Corp. The bank laid down a new policy.

It decided that it had to write off one quarter of its loans to all countries which had said they needed to reschedule their debt, reducing the interest charge or delaying the capital repayments. Where a country or company is in default on its interest payments Citi-Corp has decided to write off the whole of the outstanding loan. Citi-Corp had to write $3000 million off its loans to 30 developing countries. It meant that in a single quarter it recorded a $2500 million loss and it set a standard which many other banks are finding hard to match. The decision to write off 25 per cent of the advances to countries under rescheduling is not as prudent as it might at first seem. For where the debt of such countries is freely traded on a open market it has a value somewhere between 15 per cent and 75 per cent of its nominal value. It implies that the average discount which Citi-Corp should have applied was larger than 25 per cent. None the less, it was a bold move and one which took the world several steps nearer to honesty through its dramatic impact (*Financial Times*, 20 August, 1987).

Chase Manhattan felt called upon to match the Citi-Corp move. This entailed doubling main reserves to $2700 million, requiring an extra write off of $1600 million in one go, meaning that it lost almost $1.5 billion in the second quarter of 1987.

Bank analysts have pored over the figures ever since the Citi-Corp decision. They have estimated that Manufacturers' Hanover, with a very large outstanding series of loans to Latin America, would require four and half times its net income in 1987 to bring its provisions up to the Citi-Corp standard. Now that some banks have a bigger war chest it means that they are freer to reduce the debt outstanding to Third World countries by selling it on. Citi-Corp intends to use some of its outstanding advances to Latin American countries as the necessary asset to carry out debt-swap transactions. As it swaps its debts and achieves less than nominal value for them it will use the loan provisions it has built up.

Table 3.2, showing estimates by a variety of professional analysts, indicates the extent of the problem. The Swiss, the Germans and now the Americans are making better progress in building up reserves in relation to the exposure to Latin American loans. None the less, the American figures are still quite low as a percentage of the total risk. The Japanese, British and American banks are all heavily exposed in Latin America, as is revealed by the fact that many of them have larger loans outstanding to Latin America than they have as total equity base. At its simplest, this means that were all the Latin American loans to go wrong at the same time — a doomsday scenario — the banks would all have their equity more or less wiped out. In 1988, some banks have taken the process further, taking provision up to 40 or over 50 per cent of Third World debts.

Table 3.2: Debt structure of leading banks

Bank	Latin American loans (in $ billions)	% of total equity	Reserves as % of exposure
US			
Citi Corp	11.6	80	25
Bank of America	7.3	178	29
Chase Manhattan	7.0	190	15
Morgan Guarantee	4.6	88	20
Chemical	5.3	168	20
Manufacturers' Hanover	7.6	202	13
British			
Barclays	4.0	65	7
Lloyds	8.7	193	7
Midland	7.1	210	8
National Westminster	4.2	54	13
Japanese			
Bank of Tokyo	5.2	128.3	
Dai-Ichi	3.4	57	
Fuji	2.6	41.2	
West German			
Deutsche	3.4	40	
Swiss			
Credit Suisse	1.6	39	30

Source Salomon Bros, Keele Bruyette & Woods, IBCA via *The Economist*, 30 May 1987

Citi-Corp followed up its suprise move of increasing its reserves with another natural move, the strengthening of its equity base. Even Citi-Corp, a fairly strong bank, was left with too narrow a gap of assets over liabilities following the extra provision it had to make. So Citi-Corp decided to raise $1000 million in new equity in August of 1987. As the Federal Reserve tightened its grip and demanded a better ratio between equity and all the loans outstanding, Citi-Corp was aware that in order to improve its competitive position it needed to raise new equity money. Its move leaves Manufacturers Hanover and Bank of America quite exposed with equity ratios to their total assets of under 2.5 per cent. Citi-Corp's is now at 3.6 per cent. A more comfortable position is to have a ratio of around 4–5 per cent (*Financial Times*, 20 August 1987).

As Table 3.2 shows, in the UK, the Midland Bank was particularly heavily exposed to Third World debt, especially in Latin America. The Midland therefore decided it needed to undertake major surgery. As Midland wrestles with the inadequacy of its capital base and the problems of its Third World debt, it demonstrates just how massive the changes are that are being forced on the banking sector by the debt crisis.

In July 1987 Midland decided to raise £700 million from shareholders through a large rights issue of new shares (Midland Rights Issue Document, July 1987). It also decided it had to raise further money by selling 3 of its operational areas. Clydesdale, Northern and Northern Bank of Ireland were sold to National Australia Bank, ending Midland's unique representation in the Scottish and the Irish retail markets. Midland was paid almost £400 million for the sale of these large assets. Out of the £1100 million which Midland raised £916 million gross had to be spent immediately on increasing its level of provisions against Third World debt. By the middle of 1987 Midland had built up its total provisions for debt in 30 countries to only £271 million. Midland's decision to increase this by £916 million, took the total to £1187 million. This means that it has now provided for some 27.5 per cent of its total LDC debt compared with a tiny percentage before the fund-raising exercise. Midland will be left with a little more than these figures imply as there will be a tax benefit from making the provisions. This meant reporting a loss for 1987.

As a result of these manoeuvres Midland produces an equity to asset ratio of 4.7 per cent, much nearer the UK average of over 5 per cent and considerably stronger than many of the larger American banks like Citi-Corp and Manufacturers Hanover. It is a sign of the resolution of banks worldwide to tackle what has been a gigantic problem, that they are prepared to raise such large sums of money in one go and to apply them so liberally to improving their loss provisions.

The same story is being re-enacted in Canada. The banking regulators there in the middle of 1987 recommended more prudent guidelines. The Bank of Montreal was the first to respond lifting its reserves against loans to the most troubled debtor nations to the

35 per cent level. This cost 753 million Canadian dollars as a write off against its third quarter earnings. Toronto Dominion and Canadian Imperial Bank of Commerce have raised their provisions to the full 40 per cent of LDC debt within the guidelines of the superintendent who suggested provisions within the range of 20–40 per cent. They had to pay around 450 million Canadian dollars each from their earnings to reach this level. Overall the six largest Canadian banks can expect to spend over US $6 billion on extra provisions and can expect to see their capital shrink by some 17 per cent. The net result of all this activity must be a further flurry of share issues by Canadian banks, being led by the Canadian Imperial Bank of Commerce which raised 300 million Canadian dollars through a common stock offering (*Financial Times*, 25 Aug. 1987).

So the wheel has turned a full circle. The post-war period of expansion, which was fuelled by large American surpluses and recycled dollars flowing through the Euro-markets, has given way to a period where the world is dependent upon the large Japanese trading surpluses and yen recycled by the Japanese banks. The transition has not been smooth. The sudden cessation of American lending overseas, which came about because of America's rapid plunge into deficit, was a jolt to the system.

The inherent instability of a debt-based culture was bound to become apparent some time anyway. The Americans have been successful in lending more and more money to people. The problem was that many of the countries and corporations they lent to did not have the skills to be able to deploy the capital productively and profitably. They got themselves into more and more debt and never built up sufficient equity base to be able to withstand the pressure. The decision to go for growth was not in itself a bad one. The decision of many countries to accelerate their development programmes by borrowing money was understandable and could have worked well. But these decisions went wrong.

In part they went wrong because everyone insisted on doing it by debt rather than equity. In part they went wrong because each of the countries concerned chose state-led nationalised solutions to many of their larger development problems; the incentive and entrepreneurship needed to carry them through to success was missing. In part they went wrong because of the political and financial instability which characterised their governments' activities. As the debts built up, and as the country failed to develop the prosperity to service them and to build an equity base, so the financial systems became more and more unstable. Each government feared that the dire economic situation would lead to its downfall if it had to face elections and so each resorted to expedients. The expedient was usually a stay of execution on the existing debt and some new borrowings to tide them over. Few countries succeeded in tackling the underlying problems of unproductive and unremunerative investment and gross overgearing. Many still suffered the consequences of economic failure at the ballot box.

A way to solvency?

The impact on the banking system was dramatic. For several years after Brazil stopped paying its interest charges and after it became clear that Peru and Ecuador and others were going to have great difficulty repaying their debt, banks carried on in the belief that lending to countries was different from lending to individuals or companies and that, in due course, interest and capital would be duly repaid. It was not until the late 1980s that banks saw this was unrealistic. The beginnings of a market in Third World debt revealed just how big the effective discount was on the true value of that debt. The brinkmanship of Brazil, Mexico, Peru and others, and the eventual cessation of interest payments by countries as large as Brazil, brought home how unrealistic it was to suppose that banks could get by without writing-down or writing-off some of the debts. Banks are now slowly and painfully rebuilding their own equity capital base as they must to make their provisions adequate.

At the same time, cautiously and laboriously, the financial technology is being assembled to give the world what it needs. The world needs a large increase in its equity base. This will be achieved by making bank loans and debts into tradable securities, by debt swapping into equity and by encouraging an increase in worldwide, local and regional stock market activity, which can deliver equity into the hands of the poorer countries that need it.

The crisis scenarios that people have commonly reckoned will take place have always looked too apocalyptic. The idea that there is something virtuous in bankrupting all the banks that have made a mistake and starting again seems excessive. There is no doubt that such bankruptcies would stop any remaining inflation in the system but it would take many years to recover from the catastrophic impact this would have on world activity. There is no guarantee that, in the panic that would follow, people would not make similar mistakes in the effort to rebuild shattered economies and in the new banking institutions they set up. It seems more desirable to adjust the world as quickly as possible without encouraging a wholesale collapse in the banking system.

But austerity alone is not an attractive proposition. Considerable sacrifices have been made by many Third World countries. Latin American countries have been forced by the IMF to accept a 15–20 per cent cut in their living standards overnight in an effort to cut their import bills and to stabilise their economies. But the large debtor nations cannot be served a diet of austerity and nothing else. Their political systems will not tolerate it and they will come to see the benefits of wide-scale reneging on debt capital as well as going soft on the interest payments. There is a great deal of truth in the allegation that if you owe a bank £1 you are in its debt, but if you owe a bank a billion pounds the bank is beholden to you. This is the precarious power balance which the Latin American countries in particular are constantly exploring. These perceptions lay behind the Baker plan's attempt to go for growth with a judicious mixture of structual adjustments in return for new lending.

Nor do the schemes that amount to cancellation or reduction of the debt at the expense of the tax-payers of Western nations present an attractive way forward. Many schemes have been produced which effectively amount to converting loans into grants. But why should the tax-payers of the West bail out the banks of the West in so direct a way? Surely it makes better sense for the marketplace to apply its pressures and gradually squeeze the Western banks into doing the honourable thing, writing-down their debts and re-capitalising themselves? It is virtuous and charitable to cancel government to government loans to the dustbowl African countries: it is foolish to subsidise Western banks who have lent too much to Brazil.

The best solution lies in encouraging markets to operate. The main solutions will come from the growing involvement of the Japanese banks in financing the Third World and the switch in the financing systems from debt to equity. For this to occur the new financial technology which this book describes must be welcomed and accepted as part of the revolution of popular capitalism. The Western banks and the Western tax-payers have found to their cost in the last 20 years that trying to force the pace of development by heavy injections of loan capital through governments and state corporations simply does not work. It gives people in the developing countries inflated expectations and hopes which are then dashed in a politically damaging process. The end result is that the Western governments and banks who exported the capital in some strange way get blamed for the failure of the Third World countries to develop and respond.

The new method, of course, is not without its own hazards. The countries of the world are interdependent and there will always be political tensions between those that have most and those that have least. There will always be a role for subsidies and free gifts. In the poorest countries of all, the West does have a duty to offer free food when the harvest has failed. More importantly, it has a duty to transfer technology and offer assistance for the rebuilding of the battered east African economies.

The West must accept that as it shifts the burden of its financing from debt to equity it will develop a different kind of claim on the Third World country which is also vulnerable. In earlier periods, when equity financing was more common, the risk was that the host country would decide to nationalise or exploit the asset the Western investor had purchased. It is easy to whip up nationalistic feeling against foreign investors when a country's government is under other kinds of pressure. There will be times when Western equity investment will prove as vulnerable as debt investment.

There are, however, two main advantages in going the equity route. The first is that the claim on the country is directly related to the success of the country's economy. A major problem with debt investment is that the worse the economy performs, the higher the political and economic risk, which results in higher interest rates. As a result those countries least able to pay the interest have to pay the highest interest rate charges. This is likely to precipitate a crisis sooner rather than later, especially as the high interest charges reflect a failure to deploy the capital productively. Conversely, with equity investment, the claim on the country is directly linked to the success of the investment being made. This means that if the country spends the money foolishly there is no further claim on that country concerned and, far from compounding the problem, it makes it lighter.

The second great advantage of equity investment is that it encourages all concerned to concentrate much more upon how the investment can repay, how the enterprise can pay off. Both Western countries making the investment and the host countries receiving it will be much more concerned to ensure that the investment is well managed and meets an obvious demand in the local economy. Too many of the investments made on the back of large debts went into huge projects that absorbed large amounts of loan debt, offering prestige to the politicians receiving them and a large scale transaction to the lending bank. They were not as interested in the enterprise and its success as an equity investor naturally would be.

Above and beyond these two fundamental advantages the idea of the switch to equity is to encourage the enterprise economy. The paradox of the Third World has been that the most entrepreneurial people living there have systematically exported their capital from their own countries. They themselves have not been prepared to put up with the political instability, the chronic fiscal imbalances, the heavy indebtedness, the high interest rates to foreigners and the signs of economic failure. Their money has gone abroad. If the cult of the equity can be rebuilt foreigners and domestic individuals may begin to demonstrate that they have green fingers with equity investment. Then there is more reason why the most enterprising people in the society, the people with savings, should return to their domestic stock markets and their domestic banking system so that they themselves will have a stake in the future of their countries. It would be a good test for many potential Western equity investors in a developing country to see how much local investment will go into a given project. If no local investment is forthcoming the Western investor could well be sceptical or might decide to withdraw his generous offer because it requires backing from all sides.

The Third World debt crisis will probably pass. The banks are at least making rapid strides to broaden their base. The debtor nations have not formed a cartel to refuse to carry on with necessary payments. Plans, like the Brazilian one to convert half its US $68 billion of debt to banks into tradable securities, show a willingness to negotiate, though in this case the recommended solution was too severe. In the end bad debt will be converted into tradable securities by the marketplace itself and the first prerequisite was the rebuilding of the banks' capital base so they could withstand the extent of the losses.

The restoration of banking stability is a necessary prelude to the restoration of general stability. The world announced to the Americans in the autumn of 1987 that it was no longer prepared to finance the massive twin deficits on easy terms. A painful period of adjustment was ushered in, which should serve to even up some of the massive financial flows from surplus countries to the US. The US debt crisis is following hard on the heels of the LDC one and complicates adjustment.

4

Disencumbering the State: Privatisation on a Global Scale

Privatisation had several forerunners and antecedents. In the UK the Conservative government of the early 1970s had managed to sell a travel agency and a few pubs before the pressures to nationalise overwhelmed it. Chile witnessed a strange early flowering of popular capitalism against the backdrop of a military regime none too concerned about individual rights. In British Columbia the Social Credit party put through a pioneering sale of shares in the British Columbia Resources and Investment Corporation, only to see many shareholders burn their fingers as the new private company fell on hard times. Most would agree that the main influence and the dominant model for the rest of the world in the 1980s was the UK government's programme, pieced together after the election of 1979. Margaret Thatcher's UK government hesitantly began to return public assets to the private sector from 1979 onwards. There were few if any involved in the process who thought that the idea would be imitated worldwide. Even more remote was the idea that it would become the biggest international political phenomenon of the 1980s.

The programme began in a conventional British way as part of the ping-pong politics between Conservative and Labour administrations. In the mid-1970s Labour nationalised the ship yards and the aerospace companies: in the heat of opposition the Conservative party pledged itself to put them back into the private sector on its return to government. At the same time the Labour government made an ignominious trip to the IMF in 1976 to seek more money and was forced, in the customary way, to accept IMF advice, which entailed cutting back on the domestic budget. It is one of the important quirks of British government accounting that the sale of an asset by the public sector counts as negative public spending. The Labour government decided that one of the sacrifices they would make to

71

the IMF would be the sale of some shares in British Petroleum. This company had a substantial private sector shareholding and was one over which the government traditionally exercised little influence.

The precedent of the sale of BP shares was readily taken up by the Conservative government which found itself, in its early years, as impecunious as its Labour predecessor. The Conservative government found it difficult to implement the pledge to return the ship yards to the private sector for they were making heavy losses and were in need of massive government subsidy. But it did keep its pledge concerning the aerospace companies, selling British Aerospace to the investing public. It cautiously embarked upon a programme which included other assets, like Amersham International, the small radio chemical company that had by accident been built up in public ownership, and the National Freight Corporation, a large trucking business.

It was not until as late as 1983 that the Conservative administration in the UK, following its second important election victory, decided to embark on a bigger programme. When the idea was first mooted it was not immediately taken up. Politicians saw the advantages of having a steady source of reliable money flowing into the government coffers without having to put up taxes. They saw the advantage of having negative public spending to put into the budget to make the public expenditure figures look that much better: they were valiantly trying to control spending but without very much success. And a few of them had a vague idea that it would be better to put things into the private sector as they might function better there than they did in the public sector. But each sale was likely to be bedevilled as the previous ones had been by the tremendous inter-departmental warfare that characterises Whitehall and by the reluctance of some ministries to see their sacred cows put out to grass in private sector fields. The government accepted civil service advice that each nationalised industry would need separate legislation, thereby greatly complicating the process. It rejected external advice that enabling legislation would be possible and speedier.

None the less politicians decided to be bold and agreed that a £5000 million per annum programme was possible within three years. Over the life of the 1983–7 Parliament there was a substantial increase in the volume of assets being sold. The single most important event was the decision to sell the utility British Telecom, monopoly supplier of telephone services in the UK, by a public offer. It was during the process of selling British Telecom that the wider ownership scheme of popular capitalism was born, through the need to find a way of selling enough shares to the British public.

Meanwhile elsewhere in the world other people had been thinking along similar lines. The American administration had a known predeliction for private enterprise. It was begining to ask why it was that developing countries were not reaping the rewards from all the periods of government-to-government subsidies and loans that had characterised development economics in the previous 30 years. By late 1985 the US administration was interested in the idea of exporting privatisation to the world. In February 1986 Secretary of State George Shultz announced that US AID would encourage the idea of privatisation in each of its missions in developing countries with the hope of achieving two privatisations in each mission territory every year. This was one of the most important decisions of all in spreading the message throughout the Third World.

French opposition politicians visiting London in the mid-1980s also expressed considerable interest in what they could learn from the British experiment. French politics resembled the British scene ideologically and a new tradition was developing there that what the socialists nationalised should be privatised. The 1981 Mitterand nationalisations were felt to have gone too far, including as they did clearly viable competitive commercial banks. Many of the 1981 clutch of state enterprises kept on managers who saw their roles lying within the private sector rather than the public. Once the Chirac administration was elected in 1986 they were intellectually and technically prepared to implement a bold programme. The government showed considerable single-mindedness and firmness of purpose once elected. The managers of the recently nationalised enterprises were more than ready to collaborate.

The spread of the message to other countries was extremely uneven. The Canadians expressed considerable interest early on and the Conservative government made it one of the cornerstones of its rhetoric. However, when it came to implementation the Canadians were always far more cautious, stumbling from excuse to excuse as to why the major corporations in Canada could not be privatised yet, if privatised at all. The programme began with political infelicities, like the sale of De Havilland, Canada's leading aircraft manufacturer, to its principal US rival, Boeing. It created a large North American monopoly and offended Canadian sensibilities, always wary of extending US economic influences in Canada. None the less the Industry ministry remained the one ministry in Canada throughout the 1980s that was prepared to go private.

The Energy ministry dithered over Petrocan and even over the small radio chemical company which it saw as a useful harbinger for bigger things. The Transport department vacillated over Air Canada, although the company itself was keen to return to the private sector, and over the railways. The airports were never on the agenda. The appointment of a special minister for privatisation, Barbara McDougall, towards the end of 1986, should have presaged better things. But McDougall was also a minister for womens' affairs and these seemed of greater interest to her than privatisation. In her early months she demonstrated that it was possible for a minister of privatisation to become an obstacle rather than a help as her appointment complicated the internecine departmental warfare that characterises so many governments.

Privatisation came to Jamaica by a process of planned accidents. The US AID mission in Jamaica decided to pay for Richard Downer, a director of the National Investment Bank of Jamaica and a former adviser to the Prime Minister, to go to Washington in February 1986 to attend the first US AID conference spreading the idea of privatisation to the developing world. Richard Downer, a doughty believer in free enterprise and the powers of the market, was entirely persuaded by the arguments at the conference and returned to his country to urge more effective privatisation. Jamaica had hesitantly begun to return one or two companies to the private sector, primarily small investments made by the National Investment Bank of Jamaica. Richard Downer identified the National Commercial Bank as one of the targets which it should be possible to sell.

Downer came to London in June of 1986 for discussion of the problems, the principal one being the size of the bank in relation to the size of the domestic stock market. The value of the total bank was clearly well in excess of the annual turnover of the Jamaican Stock Exchange. There was no evidence that Jamaicans would immediately clamour to buy shares in NCB in a country where only 1 per cent of the population participated in the stock market. Downer returned to Jamaica armed with the documentation on British Telecom to see if he could persuade his colleagues that a similar popular capitalism issue could be launched on the Jamaican Stock Exchange.

I went to Jamaica in the autumn to see the progress. We sat down and thought through the problems. The Prime Minister who had some modest interest in the principle first of all needed an adequate cabinet paper setting out a possible profile for the issue with a timetable and some arguments as to why it might succeed. The first task was to draft a cabinet paper of sufficient quality. It might then carry the Prime Minister and the cabinet. The next task was to assemble a team of people who might be able to carry out a large scale divestment using a stock market which had never before seen an issue on this scale. A small team was assembled from the National Investment Bank of Jamaica (the vendor), Price Waterhouse (the consulting accountants), some of the best lawyers we could find on the island, representatives from the National Commercial Bank itself and three people from N.M. Rothchilds of London, seconded to the NIBJ for the assignment. Leading this team was a fascinating challenge. The team set itself a very tight timetable, deciding that twelve weeks from the original conception through to the close of application lists was a necessary deadline in order to sustain the momentum in a climate which could otherwise turn hostile quite quickly.

At one of the first presentations to the institutional investors the team tried the idea out on them to hear their views on the possible size of the market and the likely price of the issue. They responded politely but there was a certain scepticism in their tone. They were reluctant to admit that the market could handle an issue of the size required. At the same time they were concerned that the NIBJ would only sell half the bank leaving half in government hands as they had a natural distrust of the government. They did not wish to see the government meddling at all in a company in which they might be investing their clients' monies. They were naturally canny when it came to talking about price, as potential buyers should be, and were surprisingly vague when it came to discussions of marketing techniques and the practicalities of handling an issue on that scale within the context of the Jamaican stock market. Contingency plans had to be made to ensure that there was sufficient room in broking offices and bank branches with trained staff available to receive the applications when they came in. Because the postal system did not work very well, particularly across the Christmas period, it was decided that all of the application forms had to be handled by the bank and broking courier systems and the allotment of the share certificates was to be done using the same mechanism in reverse. Individual applicants were responsible for delivering their application forms personally to one of the 400 bank branches and broking offices around the island. Each applicant had to pick up the share certificate in person a few weeks later.

Active discussion of increasing the trading hours of the exchange from four hours a week (two hours on Tuesday and two hours on Thursday morning) did not result in any immediate extension of hours, but the pressure of transactions now resulting from the issue is likely to make it inevitable. In the second day of trading after the NCB issue the volume of trading went over one million shares in the day for the first time ever on the Jamaican exchange and brokers found, as expected, that the volume of paperwork was difficult to handle. The settlement system was already under pressure before the NCB issue, often resulting in delays of three to six months before receipt of share certificates. This was both because the stamp office was slow at processing and collecting the stamp duty payable and, more importantly, because the registrars of the companies concerned often delayed registering the stock in their share register and issuing the new or balance certificate. Similar delays were familiar in London following the explosion of trading after the 1986 deregulation of the markets!

Herculean efforts were needed to set up a computer programme that could handle 30,000–50,000 applications for shares, and to reassure the banking system that it could receive the monies, collect the interest on the capital pending the allocation of share certificates, and handle the issuing of the shares certificates. In the end all went smoothly and the whole thing reconciled to the nearest cent without a great deal of difficulty.

The Jamaican experience demonstrated that a popular capitalism issue could be launched in a developing country and the response to it was quite magnificent. It was over-subscribed by 2.7 times. Thirty thousand shareholders and an opening premium of Jamaican $1.50 over the purchase price testifies to the popular enthusiasm which gripped the Jamaican marketplace. For the first time in its history the gallery of the tiny Jamaican stock exchange, housed in the Bank of Jamaica building, was packed with people watching the hectic trading and the brokers were deluged with orders.

Elsewhere in the developing world the progress of divestment was variable, but usually centred in 1986 and early 1987 on sales of smaller industrial businesses to foreign investors or to local company and corporate investors. Senegal, Malawi, Zambia, India, Pakistan and Sri Lanka all went this route. The vogue spread to the Far East where stock markets became a recognised way of selling the privatisation issues. In Malaysia the Guthrie corporation was returned to investors through the London stock market. In Singapore, Singapore Airlines was sold to new owners in a privatisation-style issue and was one of the pioneering airlines issues. It was followed by KLM in Holland and British Airways in the UK.

The message spread quite rapidly to Japan. Japanese committees of experts visited London as early as 1984 to investigate and were particularly impressed by the large scale of the British Telecom operation. The Japanese decided to proceed on plans for the sale of all their four state enterprises — the tobacco monopoly, the state railways, the telephone company and the airline. They began with the telephone company as it was the most profitable and the most interesting, with a bright technological future ahead of it. It was to be the world's most massive issue measured by the total capitalisation of the stock undergoing treatment. The Japanese decided to do it in relatively small tranches and they succeeded in selling the first on the whopping price earnings multiple of 144 times. Priced like this the 'small' tranche was still the largest equity issue in the world! Foreigners looked on in amazement as the Japanese welcomed the shares at this level, despite the rather mediocre profit performance in previous years and the high level of the Japanese market at the time of the issue.

The decision to split the railways up into different operating companies and to split off the freight railway was pioneering work. The world is now watching to see the results of this novel privatisation. The airline was fraught with more difficulties as recent operating results had been poor and morale needed boosting after the terrible jumbo jet crash.

In New Zealand the Labour government undertook a radical experiment in free market economics. It made progress in deregulating and in rolling back the level of state intervention in the economy. It had succeeded in characterising the previous National party administration as a specialist in grandiose and often unrealistic investment projects by the state. The 'Think Big' programme of the National Party was out of favour in a big way.

It was not long before the government, particularly the finance minister Douglas, became interested in adding privatisation to the modern economic programme New Zealand was pursuing. There was an understandable reluctance on the part of a Labour administration to contemplate wholehearted 100 per cent denationalisation of some of the crown jewels of the New Zealand state. But the visiting parties to England grew more and more interested in the benefits that could accrue — the growing capital market, the better performance of managers and men, the raising of morale and the raising of money. Attention centred upon the sale of minority stakes in some of the big and profitable enterprises, particularly Petrocorp the oil producer and oil product company and ANZ the bank. Finally, in 1988, the need for cash resulted in the attempted sale of the whole of Petrocorp to a foreign predator, British Gas.

New Zealand also made rapid strides in deciding that utilities were suitable cases for treatment — something the French, the Canadians and others had rejected as being unrealistic. New Zealand put the liberalisation of its electricity board up for tender, one of the first electricity enterprises to be regarded as a suitable case for treatment in the whole of the modern wave of privatisation and liberalisation. It also looked at its forest enterprises and is currently making them more commercial. The main brunt of the New Zealand programme was called 'corporatisation' — making state industries more efficient and making them operate like private companies.

In Europe the Mediterranean countries were working out their own solutions to their problems. Both Spain and Italy had inherited from their past great rambling empires of industrial holdings conglomerated under a state holding company. ENI in Spain and IRI in Italy had once been held out as the very paragons of socialist virtue by left-wing thinkers across the world, particularly in the UK. Yet both IRI and ENI had had the same gloomy history, with loss piling on top of loss and with those at the top of their empires struggling even to keep up with the spate of annual reports and accounts that their subsidiaries and offspring spawned with monotonous regularity. It became increasingly difficult to see what the function of the holding company was and to see any redeeming merit in the system of lumping together large diverse industrial businesses under one state enterprise umbrella.

In Italy a singularly impressive man rose to the head of IRI. Professor Prodi turned himself into one of the most ambitious and effective privatisers of the world. He saw that, in order to make some commercial sense out of his straggling empire, he needed to raise money from asset sales, both to reduce the risk and complexity of his task and to get the money in to repay some of the debts which he had inherited.

Prodi was defeated on one of his early forays to try and sell the large food combine SMEE. But he was not to be permanently defeated and his finest hour came when he settled upon the idea of selling Alfa Romeo, the prodigious Italian car manufacturer. Fiat, the natural buyer within the Italian motor industry, was reluctant to play. Fiat had previously been persuaded to buy Lancia and the results had been poor. Loss had followed loss and Fiat had found it difficult to make anything of the struggling Lancia group, bedevilled as it was by a reputation for poor quality and rusty cars.

Fiat's game plan was probably to keep Alfa within the state sector. Prodi took an adventurous decision to negotiate with US companies and then went public with the idea that there would be a US takeover for Alfa Romeo. It was a calculated gamble. Fiat lobbied powerfully on the matter and went direct to the Prime Minister. In Italy politicians are noticeably weak and Prime Ministers come and go with remarkable rapidity. Coalitions briefly form and then disintegrate before any consistent decisions can be applied. Prodi stuck to his guns and as a result succeeded in forcing a bid out of Fiat, thus shedding himself of the troublesome Alfa Romeo, which had been the plaything of politicians for years. They had for example forced Alfa to locate in southern Italy to provide an answer to the difficult problems of unemployment in the Mezzo Giorno. IRI is now on the road to financial recovery with debt reduction and asset sales proceeding apace.

In Spain the authorities also decided that enough was enough with the rambling empire of ENI. Spain, too, had a troubled car industry in public ownership. The spin-off from Fiat in Spain, Seat, the manufacturer with the dominant market position, was under government control, heavily loss making and finding that its product range was dated and in difficulties. The Spaniards acted with great firmness of purpose, seeking a foreign partner and rapidly conducting successful negotiations with Volkswagen. There was far less political trouble than over Alfa Romeo in Italy, and both countries demonstrated considerable skill compared with the UK.

In the UK the negotiations over a foreign partner for British Leyland became the subject of one of those famous media hype scandals of industrial policy which led to a damaging retreat early in 1986. The loss of the negotiating position with General Motors over Leyland vehicles, trucks, buses and the other heavy vehicles producers, was damaging to the strategy of rolling back the public interest in the British motor industry.

Shortly afterwards it was revealed that secret negotiations had been going on between Austin-Rover (also part of BL) and Ford. This was an undesirable liaison anyway on competition grounds — if Ford had merged with British Leyland cars it would have had half the UK market. Retreat was inevitable in the wake of the strong lobbying that had accompanied the climb down over Leyland trucks. By the middle of 1986 the British government strategy for the motor industry was in tatters. It was one of those ironies of life that where the British government had started firmly on privatisation and had launched it in the world, it was the Spanish and Italian state enterprise holding companies that made the fast running on improving their own motor industry by inviting in foreign capital and technology or by shedding the load from the public sector to a private sector manufacturer. In 1988 the UK government recovered its poise and announced negotiations for the sale of the Rover Group to British Aerospace.

By late 1986 the fashion was such that any self-respecting country and government had to ask itself whether it too needed a privatisation programme and how such a programme might fit in with its other policies. In continental Europe privatisation was being discussed in every government centre. In Belgium, where coalition governments were constantly beset by budget difficulties, considerable research into the possibilities went on throughout 1986. Could the state holding company divest some of its holdings or even bring in private capital at holding company level? Could some of the utilities be returned to private ownership? In Germany, where the state sector was much smaller to begin with, there was modest interest and some small stakes in public enterprises were returned to the market or their sale discussed. In Austria, where elections were held early in 1987, it was confidentially assumed that once the election was out of the way the government would turn to tackling the problems of the big Austrian state holding company. Tackling the problems now meant introducing private capital and removing some of the equity from the government accounts.

In Latin America a grand clearance sale was announced in several countries, although results were often slow to follow the initial statements of intent. In Argentina, Brazil and the other heavily indebted countries dozens or hundreds of enterprises were nominally for sale, and some enterprising people came along with bids for individual ones. In each case it was a trade sale rather than a stock market placing that was undertaken. In Chile, the right-wing government, not known for its belief in the liberties of the subject, was none the less pursuing an economic policy that showed a strong belief in economic freedom. This too entailed the introduction of more private capital, with the conscious intention of building a bigger and better stock market. The building of the Chilean stock market near the centre of Santiago was itself a testament to the type of problems a developing country faced. An old building in the Victorian colonial mould, it is now badly cracked and shaken by an earthquake. But there are also signs of renewed life, as broking business picks up and people begin to reinhabit the offices and invest some money and time in the new stock market activities that are beginning to blossom.

The US administration turned out to be the most recalcitrant in implementing at home the policies which it was exporting so liberally abroad. The President appointed a privatisation adviser to his White House staff and, at various times throughout 1986, all of the possible state enterprise candidates were discussed and reviewed. Were the power board to be sold as originally promised in the 1986 budget? Would Conrail finally find an acceptable bidder? Could the petroleum reserve be privatised? By the time of the publication of the 1987 budget, at the turn of the year, opinion had hardened in favour of Amtrac and the Federal loans.

Early in 1986 there had been a brief flurry of interest in the idea that the American administration could and should sell the Washington airports. Washington National and Washington Dulles were both owned by the Federal government. Both airports suffered from many of the ills of nationalised industries elsewhere. Washington National, in particular, was run down and in need of major new investment. It had not been brought up to date, its terminal capacity was inadequate and it had missed out on many of the new services and retailing activities that are routine in more modern airports. The value of the real estate, close to the heart of Washington, had never been fully realised. The most valuable asset of all, the right to land aeroplanes, was not reflected in any pricing policy, even though there is great pressure on slots at Washington National because the airport is close to the centre of the city.

The suggestion that the Washington airports could be privatised as an example to the world and simultaneously greatly improved by the introduction of new capital, led to a political row. It was fascinating to see the centre of capitalism, busily exporting the doctrine of privatisation to the world, totally unable to handle the simple idea that two of the nation's leading airports could be sold. The Baltimore lobby were against the proposal, for Baltimore airport offers competition to the two Washington airports. The users seemed to fear that a privatised Washington would represent more effective competition. The Secretary of State for Transport, Mrs Dole, was against the proposal as she wished to minimise the amount of fuss with the lobby groups and pass the Federally-owned assets over to the state, leaving them largely untouched in the process. Some of the airlines and other users were concerned lest the true value of the landing slots at Washington National be revealed. Others signed up in favour of the proposition, seeing the opportunity for new investment, for a better airport, and for fees or profits for their businesses.

The debate was one for American interests alone as it was a matter of high American politics. Senators tried to make progress on the floor of the Senate, with proposals to offer the airports for sale instead of passing them over to the State authorities. They were unable to handle the enormous pressure of the lobby groups in favour of leaving the airports as they were, combined with the weight of the administration also seeking to block the privatisation.

The end result was not a surprise. The administration succeeded in preventing privatisation of two important national assets and thereby delayed the day when Washington National would be refurbished and rehabilitated to full modern standards. The Americans have demonstrated that the process they were trying to export to the world did have political difficulties — political difficulties which they themselves could not overcome in a relatively straightforward case. Subsequently the American government succeeded in selling Conrail, the rail company, in a well-executed privatisation. The US began to practice what it preached.

The full size of the British programme is now impressive and, as it has been underway for some eight years, it is already possible to form preliminary conclusions about its scale and its impact. Table 4.1 sets out the sales so far. This £12 billion programme is now growing at a rate of £5 billion a year. 1987/8 will be a year of major sales with further money from the sale of British Gas and the large British Petroleum issue alone grossing £8000 million.

There have also been a series of sales of subsidiaries by state companies where the proceeds have been received by the holding company itself rather than by the government. These included the sale of hotels and Sealink ferries by British Rail. British Leyland have sold Jaguar, Unipart and Leyland Bus. British Gas sold Wytch Farm whilst British Airways sold its helicopter business and British Shipbuilders sold the warship yards. This has brought in an additional £600 million to the public sector.

In most cases, following a sale, the companies have greatly improved their profit and investment performance. British Aerospace, privatised in 1981, has seen its profits more than double since then. Cable and Wireless, which welcomed the move into the private sector as a chance to strengthen its investment and activities overseas, has gone from strength to strength. In the year before privatisation it made a pre-tax profit of £64 million; now it is making

Table 4.1: UK Privatisation, proceeds from sale

Name of Sale	NET PROCEEDS (£000,000)							
	1979/80	1980/81	1981/82	1982/83	1983/84	1984/85	1985/86	1986/87
Amersham International			64					
Associated British Ports				46		51		
British Aerospace		43					346	
British Petroleum	276		8		543			
British Gas								1796
British Gas Debt								750
British Airways								415
British Sugar Corporation			44					
British Telecom						1352	1246	1084
British Telecom Loan Stock						44	61	53
British Telecom Preference Shares								250
Britoil				334	293		426	
Cable and Wireless			181		263		571	9
Enterprise Oil						382		
National Enterprise Board	37	83	2			142	30	
National Freight Consortium			5	33				
North Sea Oil Licences		195				121		
Miscellaneous	57	84	189	75	43	40	22	
Totals	370	405	493	488	1142	2132	2702	4357

Source: HM Treasury, Public Expenditure, White Paper

profits in excess of £300 million. Amersham International has been similarly successful with its profits expanding from £4 million in the year prior to privatisation to over £17 million in the most recent completed year. Most dramatic of all has been the surge of profitability of the National Freight consortium following the management and employee buy-out. In the last full year before purchase by the employees it made £4.3 million. It is now making more than £40 million, a tenfold expansion of its profitability in a seven year period. This has resulted in massive appreciation of the shares bought by the managers and employees and has reaffirmed the incentive and the morale-boosting impact that a management and employee stake can create in a humdrum business.

The spur of privatisation has also enabled several companies to be turned round quite effectively by their managements. British Airways was losing over £200 million at the end of the 1970s. It is now making profits in excess of £200 million and has seen steady progress, with loss reduction in 1981 and 1982 followed by the breakthrough into profit from 1983 onwards. The management, under Lord King, were convinced that offering the employees and managers the prospect of a share stake and the opportunity to move into the commercial sector was an important part of the task of galvanising them to turn the airline into a successful operation.

Jaguar cars has had a similar experience. Losing substantial amounts of money in the early 1980s, from 1982 onwards, under the leadership of John Egan, it moved into profit. By 1985 profits were over £100 million, the level necessary to sustain the investment in marketing a new product that such a company requires to succeed. Again John Egan would say that privatisation was important in persuading the workforce that Jaguar would no longer be encumbered with the problems of living within the large British Leyland conglomerate. The results are testimony to his leadership and to the incentive which shareholding and freedom have brought to the Jaguar workforce. It has not guaranteed Jaguar a strike-free future, for the employees stake is still not large compared to that of the employees of National Freight. The important consideration was to give Jaguar a separate identity so that its workforce could believe in its product, its sales performance and its investment programme. This sense of identity and shared endeavour delivered the profits which have enabled the company to modernise its production processes. It is also investing in its workforce with an attractive programme of training and educational facilities for employees at all levels.

The large utilities have been in the private sector a shorter period of time and are subject to much more stringent price control than their predecessor nationalised industries. None the less they are already showing signs of improving efficiency which is boosting profitability. British Telecom has moved off the plateau of profits of around £1000 million which it sustained in the last three years prior to privatisation, and has made steady progress up to the £2000 million mark in the last three years. British Gas showed decent profit growth in its first full year in the private sector.

The only exceptions to the rule that privatisation brings dramatic profits turnround or acceleration of growth lies with the oil companies. Britoil was privatised for the 1982 profit year. In its last full year as the British National Oil Corporation in the public sector it made profits of £437 million. Its profits have risen since then, but not dramatically, because the main determinant of profitability is the oil price and the oil price has been extremely erratic. The same is true of Enterprise Oil. In its last full year in the public sector it was making profits well over £80 million (this is the eight month figure). By 1985 the profits had risen to £138 million but they have subsequently declined quite sharply as a result of the fall in the oil price.

The pace has quickened in 1987/8, not only in terms of the amount of money raised but also the number of assets for sale. The year began in April with the sale of the Royal Ordnance factories. This sale was dogged by bad luck. The original intention had been to sell this collection of armaments manufacturers as a single corporate entity to a wider shareholding public. This ambition had floundered with difficulties over assembling a full run of figures over past years and with management problems. In April 1987 the Gordian knot was cut by the sale of Royal Ordnance to British Aerospace, for consolidation with its own aerospace defence business.

In May it was the turn of Rolls Royce. The aero-engine maufacturer had come into public ownership 14 years earlier under a Conservative administration, when it fell into great financial difficulties through a single contract for the RB211 jet engine. The financial problems were sorted out during its period of public ownership through a kind of liquidation process. The car side had already been split off as a private company.

In June it was the turn of British Gas. This was a huge sale and another important step towards bringing a large number of new shareholders into the UK market. In July the British Airports

Authority was privatised by a public offer for sale, following the re-election of the Conservative government on 11 June. The British Airports Authority owns most of the principal UK airports, including the three large London airports, Gatwick, Heathrow and Stansted. Also in July the National Seed Development Council and Plant Breeding Institute was sold to the private sector chemical industry. The intention is to use more of the ideas developed in that institute for commercial purposes, by linking them directly with a major chemical investment group.

Throughout the year various National Bus Company subsidiaries were sold, often to their managements and employees on a buy-out basis. In October 1987, the largest-ever equity offering of the programme so far, the sale of the remaining 31 per cent of British Petroleum owned by the government, took place.

The British programme has pioneered many of the techniques and breakthroughs in the privatisation process. There has been a great deal of financial innovation. It has seen the first partly-paid share issues in the public sector. In order to spread the burden of raising large amounts of capital from the market, shares were often sold with a first payment representing only a portion of their true value. Several months later a subsequent payment or payments are made to make up the full price. Privatisation has seen the introduction of competitive underwriting quotes where before, in the UK market, there was an agreed price that applied to all underwritings. This became too expensive given the large scale of the equity offerings undertaken by the government.

Privatisation has also brought experimentation with tender issues. One of the early political problems in the process was inaccurate pricing. The Amersham issue, for example, was greatly under-priced and there was a fierce debate in the House of Commons about public assets being given away too cheaply. In contrast the Britoil issue was over-priced, as the issue was damaged by a deterioration in the oil market and by statements from Saudi Arabia at a delicate time. The adoption of a partial or complete tender is the way to offset complications over selecting the right price. The 1982 issue of Britoil shares, the 1983 issues of BP shares and of Cable and Wireless shares and the 1984 issues of Associated British Ports and Enterprise Oil were based on the tender principle. In this system it is incumbent on the purchasers to write in the value they ascribe to the shares they wish to buy. The allocators of shares can then decide whether they are going to allocate down to the lowest price, which guarantees the sale of the whole, allowing everyone to purchase at that minimum price, or whether they are going to conduct a tender where people obtain shares at the actual price they specify. Both systems have been tried, and both systems succeed in avoiding allegations of gross under-pricing.

In Jamaica the issue of Caribbean Cement shares pioneered the technique of enabling the government to raise money for the assets being sold and at the same time gave the company access to new funds a year in the future. A warrant was issued with shares purchased entitling the holder to subscribe for new shares at a specified date. This capital will be used by the company as part of its expansion programme. The UK programme has occasionally raised money for the company at the same time as proceeds for the government. This was done in the case of British Aerospace, for example, which needed new capital for its own investment purposes.

The French programme is important for its firmness of purpose and the speed of its legislative process. Whereas in the UK every major sale requires a separate piece of legislation, which can take up to 18 months to draft and negotiate through the Houses of Commons and Lords, the French took enabling powers in one go at the beginning and are now able to sell as and when they wish, as financial circumstances permit. They have adopted many of the practices of the British programme, laying particular emphasis upon the mass-marketing techniques to boost the size of the stock market and bring new savers into the ownership process.

In 1987 the French programme raised 60 billion French francs and was seen by the Prime Minister, Chirac, as a prodigious social reform. The programme is tackling only the large competitive industrial and financial businesses. There are enough of those in France to keep the programme going for several years without having to encounter the difficulties the British have encountered with privatising large public utility monopolies.

The programme has not avoided all controversy. The French government, like many others, was concerned about possible hostile takeovers of newly privatised companies, especially by foreigners. Not content with the British idea of the Golden share or blocking mechanism, the French also decided to allocate certain shareholdings to friendly 'well intentioned' companies. Somewhere between 6 per cent and 25 per cent of the shares of groups privatised so far have been allocated to these core shareholders (Noyaux durs), often themselves companies undergoing privatisation and under government influence. This has led to allegations of favouritism in allocation, especially where the issues were attractively priced. It removes one pressure from the new companies, but leaves unresolved the long-term question of what happens to these concentrated shareholdings. It would be an irony if, in due course, one of these core shareholders has to sell or demands the right to sell and this very block became a starting point for a bid. The French would have been better off trusting the market or relying on a British golden share, which the government can use to stop any takeover it does not like.

The issue is especially important in the case of TFI, the TV channel, where Bouygues hold 25 per cent. This stake could be used in the future to gain major leverage over the editorial stance of the station.

Table 4.2: French privatisations

Company	Date	Market Capitalisation (Fr francs)	Individual Shareholders in Public Offer	Main Core Shareholders
Saint Gobain	Nov 1986	13.5bn	1.54m	BNP, Suez
Paribas	Jan 1987	17.5bn	3.81m	Total, UAP
Credit Commercial de France	April 1987	4.4bn	1.65m	CGE, MGF Lafarge, Coppee
Compagnie Generale D'Electricité	May 1987	20.6bn	2.24m	Société Generale, UAP, Generale des Eaux
Havas	May 1987	6.4bn	0.73m	Société Generale, Lyonnaise des Eaux, Paribas
Société Generale	June 1987	21.5bn	2.3m	AGE, CGE, GAN, Rhone-Poulenc
TFI (TV)	June 1987	3.5bn	0.42m	Bouygues
Suez	Oct 1987	20.0bn		Elf Aquitaine, Exor, St Gobain, Pernod-Ricard

Source: *Financial Times* 7 October 1987

Certain themes worldwide have sparked more interest than others. The idea of a privatised airline has caught on rapidly. Sixty-six per cent of Japan Airlines, 37 per cent of Singapore Airlines, 100 per cent of British Airways, 61 per cent of KLM and 30 per cent of MAS have been transferred from the public to the private sectors. Air Lanka, Air New Zealand, Australia Airlines, Israel's

El Al, Mexicana, Australia's Quantas, THY of Turkey and Air Canada are all under discussion in their respective countries. Banks are also a popular area for privatisation. The UK had no nationalised banks so this is an area which has been pioneered by France and Jamaica. The successful sale of Paribas and of the National Commercial Bank of Jamaica have shown the way. Austria is now contemplating a partial sale of Lander Bank, Belgium is considering selling the Office Central Du Credit Hypothecaire, IRI in Italy is introducing private capital into the Banca Commerciale Italiana, the Credito Italiano and the Banco Di Roma.

Many countries have also been interested in selling off their media businesses. The newly elected Social Democrat government in Lisbon is going to sell five state-owned newspapers and a radio station. At the same time it intends to open new television stations to private bidders. The French have embarked upon the introduction of more private ownership and capital into their television industry and the Jamaicans are contemplating the Jamaican Broadcasting Corporation as a possible privatisation candidate. This has always been seen as much more dangerous in the UK. The powerful vested interests of the British Broadcasting Corporation have succeeded in blocking any meaningful moves towards the privatisation of the two main publicly owned television channels.

In Peru the government is trying to join the bandwagon by selling its airline and is also considering bank nationalisation. Free enterprise has found a powerful voice in Mario Vargasllosa. He sees bank nationalisation as the thin end of the wedge of authoritarian control of Peruvian society. In an interview he said: 'this measure can corrupt and destroy this democracy. This is a fragile democracy in a country with enormous social and economic differences, a country without democratic traditions, where institutions are only starting to become democratic.' He sees a direct threat in state control of the banks, which would give the government control of credit. He went on to say: 'for instance, the media cannot survive as independent media if the government has total control of credit'.

In the large scale Portuguese programme the targets are all those profitable companies where capital could be easily privatised. The Prime Minister has included the state-owned breweries, the tobacco company, the cement manufacturers, pulp companies and perhaps the banks. His initial intention, like the New Zealand Labour Party's, is to sell only minority shareholdings. A similar interest in selling minority shares is developing rapidly in Finland. The first ones likely to experience this new departure are Valmet, the metals and engineering group and Kemira, the chemicals and fertiliser company.

The programmes around the world draw heavily upon the British and more recently the French experiences. In practically every country, whatever the hue of the government, the idea of involving employees and managers directly in the shareholding of the company for which they work is popular. The Turks have expressed enthusiasm, the New Zealanders and Australians see it as a way of socialising privatisation, it has been crucial in the Jamaican experience and is being contemplated in all the major European countries going this route. A second theme is the improvement privatisation might produce in economic performance at the factory and company level. People see that motivation does improve and that the freedom to develop the business in the way the management judges best can add considerable value. The only area where many countries are worried about following the British example is the privatisation of monopolies.

Britain began this course by selling British Telecom. There was a long debate prior to the sale over the best way to control the powerful monopoly that was being delivered into private hands. One school of thought believes that the only answer to the problems of monopoly lies in the introduction of a large measure of competition. With this in mind large sections of British Telecom operations were, over a period of years, completely deregulated. Anyone can now sell equipment to add on to a phone network, as long as the equipment meets specified British standards. People can now apply for a licence to provide value-added network services over the basic British Telecom network. For example, a data communication company can pay British Telecom for use of the lines and sell the service at its own price adding the value of data transmission. Finally, a complete rival network was licenced in the form of Mercury. This now offers a range of routings and services, primarily to business customers. Competition is also being intensified by the provision of two alternative networks of cellular radio phones. One, run by Racal Vodafone, is entirely separate from British Telecom, the other Cellnet, is partly owned by British Telecom.

Where this competitive edge has been introduced it has certainly worked. The range and variety of equipment supplied to add on to the network has increased dramatically. British Telecom's share of the market has dropped quite rapidly but the market has expanded enormously. The price of equipment has fallen visibly. The introduction of business line competition has lowered the price of the typical business call and has improved the efficiency of the service. Intense competition to provide car radio phones has led to a reduction in prices and a rapid expansion of the service.

The second approach to the problem of a private monopoly was to introduce clear regulation. The British hit upon a new formula. Instead of going for the very complicated rate of return on capital controls used by the private American utilities, the British opted for a formula which tried to control prices. The RPI-X approach means that British Telecom can only put up its average prices by 3 percentage points less than the standard rate of inflation in any given year. Within a general basket of services that are subject to this control, British Telecom has some freedom to increase prices for parts of the services more rapidly than others.

This approach has been very successful in curbing the rapid real price increases which British Telecom imposed on its customers in the 1970s when it was a public monopoly. It has produced two problems, however. The first is that the rebalancing of tariffs has meant that people have to pay much more for local calls, offsetting some of the benefits of much cheaper long distance calls. This mirrors the fact that there is effective competition on the long distance and not on many of the local services. The second is that the quality of service has become a highly contentious issue. The indicators produced by British Telecom and by the independent Office of Telecommunications, their watchdog, suggest that service quality has not deteriorated. Nor, however, has it improved in many areas and public expectations of what should be achieved seem to be rising all the time. As a result some have argued that the private monopoly has failed to improve service quality and that this is a direct result of it being a private monopoly. The truth seems to be that it is a direct result of it being a monopoly, whether it be publicly or privately owned.

The ramifications of this complicated story have yet to be unravelled in many countries. The result is that many governments have decided that it simply is not worth the bother of privatising a monopoly and trying to work out ways of regulating or deregulating to produce the necessary results. None the less, the strand of policy which opens British Telecom to much more competition has been most influential around the world. Many Telecom concerns are now looking at just this kind of operation and the idea of deregulating is spreading to other public utilities, most notably to electricity.

Britain compounded the problems it was experiencing in

privatising monopolies by privatising the Gas monopoly with practically no competition being introduced at all. The structure adopted for the British Gas Sale contains the seeds of dissension. As a direct result of growing public concern about privatised monopolies there is, at the time of writing, a crucial debate under way in the UK about how to privatise the electricity industry. Those arguing that electricity can only be privatised if the generation side of the activity is made fully competitive, are finding it much easier to argue their case given the experience of Telecom and Gas. Electricity is one of the easiest public utility monopolies to privatise whilst introducing substantial competition. There is no element of natural monopoly in generation whatsoever and generation accounts for 80 per cent of the total cost of electricity. The unit of generation is the 1000 megawatt station. In a country like Britain, requiring over 70 megawatts of capacity, there is ample scope for having competing generators and still reaping considerable economies of scale while covering the necessary business overheads. The government has indicated that it means to break the generating monopoly.

Privatisation is sweeping the world. It is the answer to the prayers of impecunious governments who do not wish to put up taxes or cut welfare programmes. It is liberation for managers and employees sick and tired of having their businesses run by remote control from a central government bureaucracy, all too willing to intervene but all too reluctant when it comes to taking the blame. It has fuelled a great deal of thinking about necessary restructuring of clumsily managed industries. It has opened up a whole debate about how many services need to be monopolies and how competitive pressures can be introduced. In many parts of the world, privatisation is both part of the process of democratising wealth, of broadening and deepening stock markets, and part of the process by which the government tries to get itself out of heavy indebtedness. The following chapters will examine the progress of stock markets and of debt reduction under the powerful stimulus of large scale privatisation programmes.

5

Financial Technology for Recovery: Rescheduling, Debt Swap and the Rebuilding of the Banking System

Debt swap

The headlong rush to lend money to developing countries in the late 1970s and early 1980s was followed by a hangover. As the international banks around the world looked at their over-stretched balance sheets and thought about the consequences if any of those countries should renege on the repayments or go slow on paying the interest they realised they had a problem. There were large shock waves to the system created by the Mexican crisis of 1982, when Mexico talked of reneging on its obligations and forced rescheduling upon the banks. The American deficit meant that there was little capital available to export, for the US economy was beginning to require prodigious quantities of money from around the world to pay for its ever-growing balance of payments and budget deficits. Against this background, it was scarcely propitious for Third World delegations to arrive in New York demanding easy terms and rescheduling of their debts, nor to arrive in Washington demanding still larger aid packages to see them over a difficult time.

Many of those concerned with the problem in the early 1980s favoured a market solution. If there were banks that held debt they were now unhappy with, and if there were banks that held far too much debt in their portfolios, the answer, surely, was to find a way for them to sell it on to somebody who would be less embarrassed by holding it.

The initial response to this market approach was one of fear. The market value of the debt the banks were holding as assets was going to be substantially below the face value of the debt and, in most cases, substantially below the valuation at which the banks held it on their balance sheets. The banks themselves, and the wise

93

men of the international authorities, were concerned lest the establishment of a market in debt would establish prices for debt which would make the banks write-down their assets substantially. This would expose the fundamental weakness of their balance sheets and, in some cases, imply that they were bankrupt. It was this fear above all else which powered the search for alternative solutions. The great rescheduling movement was born. IMF and World Bank programmes aimed at retrenchment for the Third World in a hectic endeavour to bring their balance of payments back into balance, and to find the wherewithal within stretched national budgets to service and repay the debt.

Huge amounts of time and energy were spent throughout the 1980s in the arduous business of rescheduling debts. At regular intervals the debtor nations had to sit down with their bank managers to discuss the basis on which they could go on servicing the debt and the possible rescheduling of the term structure of the debt, giving them more time before they had to repay. The IMF's proposals always centred around deflation, tight control of the money supply and substantial reductions in the living standards of those in the countries concerned.

But you cannot keep a good idea down and you cannot stop market practitioners practising their craft. Despite the efforts at rescheduling and the endless negotiations, banks still wanted to cut their losses on some of the debt they held as assets in their portfolios. As each year advanced more banks had written-down more of the loans in their portfolios, but they needed to make the adjustment over a period of years so that the shock to their balance sheets and their profit and loss accounts would be less dramatic than it would have been had they taken the prudent decision when the crisis first surfaced in 1982. Gradually a market was established in the debt of some of the important borrowing nations. Chile was a pioneer, keen on the idea of reducing the amount of its foreign obligations by a patient but consistent process of whittling away at the foreign borrowings it had taken out. Mexico too became seriously interested as part of the solution to its burgeoning debt problem.

The mechanism of a debt swap is not easy to explain. In the early days those banks involved in marketing it concealed it in a barrage of technical prose and focused their explanation upon a few well-briefed officials from the central banks of the leading countries concerned. Yet the principle that underlies it is, as so often with a good idea, breathtakingly simple. If there are banks that have lent too much money to countries now not thought to be very credit-worthy, and if those banks wish to get rid of the obligation, then the banks that made the loans should be prepared to take a discount in order to sell. This discount then becomes a source of value to entice a new investor to take a different kind of claim or obligation on the country that needs the money.

If a bank is prepared to sell its Mexican or Chilean debt for some 60 cents for every dollar it is owed, then the question arises as to who should pocket the other 40 cents in the event that the country finally meets its obligations. The art of debt swapping is to apportion this additional 40 cents in a reasonable way between the possible claimants, and to ensure that both the government debt overseas is cancelled and a new investor is brought in who will have some commitment to the host country's economy.

The simplest kind of debt swap is one where a foreign company wishes to make a new investment in a debtor country. The foreign company has hard currency earnings from its other international activities which it wishes to invest. If it wishes to invest US $10 million in, say, Chile, then it is in a position to buy US dollar Chilean debt from the banks that no longer wish to hold it. The company comes to an arrangement with the central bank of Chile whereby the latter agrees to make available local currency for the new investor. In return the new investor buys Chilean government debt and arranges for its cancellation through the central bank.

The debt swap agent is therefore charged with the task of buying around US $15 million of Chilean government debt for the US $10 million that the investor wishes to commit to the country. The agent then takes this debt to the Chilean central bank and it is cancelled in return for US $15 million worth of Chilean currency being issued to the new investor. In the process a commission is payable to the banks and the debt swap agent involved and the central bank of Chile itself might take 5 per cent out of the discount available on the purchased foreign debt. The balance of the profit on the transaction is an inducement to the foreign investor.

In return for getting this premium on his local investment the overseas investor has to promise to forego dividends in the early years of the project and to keep the investment in Chile for a specified number of years before he can think of repatriating the capital.

This transaction has achieved many things in one go. First it has reduced the Chilean government's obligation to pay interest on the debt thereby helping the cash flow of the government and removing some of the foreign exchange strain on the balance of payments. It has brought a new investor into the Chilean economy and given that investor some free Chilean currency to cut his risks and to act as an inducement to him. It has swapped overseas debt which may be repayable soon and which has a high interest charge on it for a longer-term equity obligation where dividends cannot be paid in the first instance. Dividends will only be paid subsequently if a productive investment is made which, in its turn, is revenue earning. The capital cannot be repaid until a reasonable number of years have passed. The obligation overseas has thus been funded long for the first time. It has also served to reduce Chile's borrowing relative to its equity and asset base and has made a small contribution to improving, rather than worsening, Chile's credit rating.

This principle is now being applied on a worldwide scale. Aquino's regime in the Philippines is a keen exponent of the powers of debt swap to reduce the enormous liabilities of her country. It is being applied throughout Latin America and will doubtless spread to other African and Far Eastern territories.

When the idea was first launched in Jamaica in the August of 1986, there was polite interest in the concept, but at that stage many Jamaicans felt it sounded technical and of no particular relevance to themselves. Jamaica is a country saddled with a very large debt burden. It owes some US $3 billion overseas with a population of only 2 million. It has one of the highest ratios of debt service to overseas earnings and of total debt to population of any of the heavily indebted countries. Some $390 million worth of the debt is money advanced by commercial banks to the Jamaican government. The bulk of the remainder is IMF and World Bank funding.

The country has been under continuous pressure from the IMF and World Bank to cut back, because some 40 per cent of the Jamaican government budget is now absorbed in debt service. The result has been a squeeze on the social and industrial programmes of the Jamaican government as the debt service charge has gone on rising through the logic of compound interest. As it becomes more difficult to foot the bill for the Jamaican debt so the interest rate charge rises as people think the risk of the country has increased. The international climate of very high interest rates overall has made the position worse. The government has tried its best to meet IMF requirements and, as a result, has had to make 10 per cent cuts in its discretionary programmes, reducing the quality of the welfare, health and other important services run by the government in order to meet the pressure of ever-rising interest costs on the debt. The politics of this is of course bad. The Jamaican government was therefore persuaded that it should explore the possibility of debt swaps.

There were those who argued that the scale of the Jamaican debt and the fact that much of the debt was owing to the World Bank and the IMF made debt swaps operating on the US $390 million of private bank advances to Jamaica an inappropriate method of proceeding. Work was done on the possibility of finding a method for funding the monies advanced by the IMF and World Bank. However, one irreducible stumbling block always remained. Neither the IMF nor the World Bank were interested in admitting that the value of their debt was other than its face value. Unless it was possible to buy the debt below its face value it was unlikely that any foreign investors would be found who would take the debt over and fund it long. The Jamaican government found its energies and time greatly absorbed by the need to renegotiate and reschedule. A sizeable amount of the money passing out across the exchanges took the form of capital repayments rather than merely interest charges.

The first task was to work out the profile of the Jamaican debt. The records of the Bank of Jamaica had to be assembled in usable form, putting together the term structure, the interest rates and the names of the leading banks. The next task was to prepare the basic documentation to enable the central bank to handle the task of cancelling bought-in debt and issuing Jamaican dollars or Jamaican assets against it.

The main policy question raised by a debt swap is the relationship between the debt swap operation and the monetary and counter-inflationary policy being pursued. If money is brought in by foreign investors and domestic currency issued against it without any other action being taken, the process can be inflationary. Of course, if there are spare resources in the economy and these resources can be put to work by the new monies then the process would be non-inflationary. If the central bank takes off-setting action in the money markets to mop up extra liquidity then the impact of the domestic currency issue can be neutralised. If the debt swap is backed by a privatisation then it is entirely non-inflationary as long-term assets are being surrendered in return for cancellation of the debt. In each debt-swap case the central bank and government have to consider the extent to which they will allow money policy to be loosened by the debt swap operation and the likely impact the release of more domestic currency will have on resources within the domestic economy.

The process in Jamaica was greatly speeded by the community of interest that was soon established. The American banks that owned Jamaican debt were already, by late 1986, interested in persuading the Jamaican government that it was a good idea, and they were beginning to line up potential investors who could take the debt off them as they clearly indicated they wished to reduce their commitment to Jamaican debt in total. Several banks were interested in pursuing business as advisers to central banks on debt swap mechanisms and they too spent considerable energy explaining to the Jamaican government how the process might work. The Prime Minister became convinced because he saw in the debt swap mechanism an opportunity for improving the balance of payments, removing some of the political pressure on his government from Washington and doing something, however modest, to ease the debt pressure. The central bank saw it was an interesting avenue as an adjunct to their endless rescheduling and general economic negotiations with the World Bank and the IMF.

It was this community of interest which led to the establishment of a task force to carry out the debt swap mechanics. The principles behind the debt swap tackled the direct causes of heavy indebtedness and the difficulty in the developing world of breaking out of the vicious circle. Successful debt swap operations first reduce the amount of borrowing relative to the amount of equity in the economy. Secondly, they can bring in new, much needed investment capital, which may then provide the stimulus needed for successful export-led industries. Thirdly, if the debt swap is linked to a privatisation, not only is it guaranteed to be non-inflationary, but it may be linked to a process which brings new technology and management into a nationalised industry which had not been working well. This can mean that the debt swap privatisation produces a better economic performance from a given public enterprise as it passes into private control and its balance sheet is restructured.

Very often the process of debt swap may entail the reduction of advances made by commercial banks to public enterprises as well as to the government itself. Complications arise when there are loans outstanding from a whole range of commercial banks, sometimes covered by different rescheduling agreements, with the advances being outstanding to the government itself, a public enterprise with a government guarantee, or to the public enterprise on its own. A rescheduling agreement will usually take precedence over any previous rules concerning the loan and its status. It becomes more difficult when some of the debt is rescheduled and some is not.

Many public enterprises in developing countries have been used as conduits for governments to borrow money from the commercial banking sector. Whilst originally there were individual projects, proposed in expectation of a good economic return, underlying these advances, most of these specific assets have got lost in a general lien on the total assets of the business or on the government itself. A successful debt swap privatisation would succeed in rationalising the complicated debt structure of the public enterprise. It would reduce central government debt, it might reduce the amount of debt outstanding by the nationalised industry subject to a government guarantee, and it should also improve the balance sheet of the public concern.

One of the functions of debt swap privatisation is to transfer assets from the public to the private sector where they might be better managed whilst tackling the accumulated burden of interest charges on that asset. The assets of many public enterprises have been over-burdened with debt. This may reflect the fact that the original project was never as viable as people thought and that the capital was over-provided. There was a tendency to gold-plating in many development schemes. It may also reflect the subsequent lack of profitability of the assets leading to the need for more borrowing to keep the business going through 'a difficult patch'. In order to give the business a chance this debt has to be removed. The central government in each country is not in a strong enough financial position to be able to cancel the debt itself. In consequence it has to bring in the commercial banks and the debt swap teams to be able to carry out this necessary debt reduction. In the developed world, where nationalised industries have often experienced similar difficulties in remunerating their capital, central governments have simply written the debt off at various times when the accumulated burden has become too great.

In July 1987 Bolivia demonstrated a new flexibility in debt swap when it linked it to what amounts to a form of country aid. Bolivia sold a slice of its debt at a discount in return for a promise to protect its rain forests. The international conservation movement persuaded Western governments that this was something worth purchasing. Bolivia is seeking to buy in all its US $1 billion of outstanding commercial debt. At the current level of discount, a massive 85 per cent, this would only cost it US $150 million. The very high level of discount reflects the stop on payments which has been declared. Chile's programme now aims to swap 15 per cent of its US $21 billion of debt by the end of 1988. Mexico has ear-marked US $2 billion of debt to be swapped in the same year. Both Chile and Mexico have a very high level of foreign debt in relation to their total national income: in the case of Chile its foreign debt amounts to 120 per cent of its gross national product, meaning that its debt interest charges absorb a very high proportion of its export earnings.

Whilst this solution has many attractions it does not always meet with political acceptance in the heavily indebted countries. Brazil's parliament voted to veto all swaps of foreign debt into direct instruments. Brazil resents the idea that an outstanding loan can be converted into some kind of equity claim on the Brazilian economy. Brazilian politicians have often seen the short-term desirability of making strident attacks upon international organisations, especially the IMF. Brazil has said that there has been too much austerity. It is therefore disappointing that many politicians in Brazil are also resisting a sensible alternative to the usual IMF package of cutting domestic demand in order to divert resources into exports. For debt swap, when it substitutes direct equity instruments in the hands of the foreigners, can be linked to raising new foreign capital to invest in the country and can become part of an economic policy based on growth. Given the attractiveness of many of the discounts on debt, a discount created by the poor economic policies of the host country, when Brazil strikes its pose against debt swap it seems to be turning down one of the best solutions on offer.

There is an irony in two elements of the modern financial technology. The management or employee buy-out of the public or private enterprise that has not done well means that the employees and managers reap what they have sown in their previous bad stewardship. The worse the management and the results, the lower the price when they come to mount the buy-out. The worse the results and the more obvious the errors, the easier it is to turn the business round. Once the turnround takes place the dramatic improvement in results is reflected quite quickly in a major improvement in value.

The same is true at the country level. The worse the record of the countries' economic management, the higher the perceived risk of holding its debt, the more potential sellers there will be. If the country has gone the way of Bolivia, Peru or Brazil and has actually tampered with interest payments or put a stop on payments under its loan agreements, the discount on the debt in the free market will be proportionately much greater. If the country then turns to a joint policy of cancelling its debt by allowing a market in it to develop and pursuing a better fiscal and monetary policy, the country, like the management in a buy-out, could reap quite rapid benefits from the turnround it is inspiring.

To date there are no examples of countries which have managed to engineer as dramatic an improvement as this would suggest. The reason is that no country in a heavily indebted position has developed the political stability and cohesion at government level to operate in the same self-interested way as a compact management and employee team can in a public enterprise being bought out at a discount. Debt-swap programmes are taking time to put in place and to get under way. Part of the reason is the complexity of the process, given the number of people and institutions which have to be involved in a successful one. The previous chapter showed how the process affects the banks themselves. It was not until 1987 that many banks had the reserves to be able to take the losses that extensive debt swapping would entail. Banks themselves have been subject to grave doubts about how much of this debt they wish to put into the marketplace and this has acted as a supply-side constraint. They are also naturally reluctant to take action to encourage cessation of interest or capital repayments. The conditions are now uniquely favourable to a major explosion in debt swap activity. Many of the early problems with the technology have been ironed out. The extensive programmes in Chile, Mexico and the Philippines have shown the different ways rules can be imposed upon debt-swap machinery and applications can be considered reasonably quickly. Now that there is a ready pool of debt in the hands of banks who have the money and the will to start realising their losses, and now that there are countries around the world beginning to understand the advantages of a debt swap programme, we should expect to see a rapid quickening of the pace.

The Philippine, Chilean and Mexican schemes differ in detail, but all have had to address themselves to certain major points. Do they allow debt swap into a privatisation? It may solve the problem of inflation inherent in a debt swap system but it also raises other matters of national policy, particularly the desirability of allowing foreigners direct access to state assets, often perceived in local terms as the core of the local economy. Secondly, where the debt swap hinges upon drawing a new foreign currency investor into the country, what rules should be developed, if any, to control his entry to given markets in the host economy and, more particularly, to control the repatriation of his profits? The main malpractice the debt swap system must guard against is the creation of a simple money-making machine for footloose hard currency investors. If the hard currency investor were allowed to put his money into the domestic economy, collecting a 30-40 per cent discount on the way, and were then able to sell up his business after a few months and take his money out of the country quite freely, the unscrupulous could use debt swap as a means of capturing for themselves the discount available. If, on the other hand, the host country both prevents the repatriation of the capital at any point in the future and imposes draconian restraints on dividend remittances from the business created, the foreign investor may be put off altogether.

No foreign investor wishes to feel completley locked into an investment in a country with high political and economic risk. There has to be a trade-off between the different objectives of the different partners. A successful scheme has to allow the hard currency investor some convertibility rights to enjoy a slice of the income generated from his new investment to be repatriated. It also has to allow the possibility, at some date in the future, of repatriating the capital. At the very least it has to allow the individual or company investor the right to switch his investment within the host economy. But here it may have to prevent him switching out of an industrial asset into a fairly safe deposit or high-yielding bond.

These are problems which countries have solved in their own different ways. The degree of freedom or constraint imposed on the new investor will reflect national policy priorities and a perception of how attractive or unattractive the prospect of becoming a debt swap investor in that country might be. As the process accelerates the balance of power may switch towards the investors, because more and more countries wish to undertake debt swap, or it may switch towards the host countries. If the former turns out to be the case a greater relaxation of the rules concerning the payment of dividends and the repatriation of capital is to be expected. If, instead, the banks prove aggressive in wishing to liquidate their high risk debt portfolios, and foreign investors are alert to the resulting discounts, the rules may be tightened by the host economies.

The situation is also affected by the attitude of central banks in the countries of origin to the banks that own the debt to be swapped. The Bank of England and the Federal Reserve are introducing new controls which entail placing usual banking ratios onto the convertible swap portfolios. Banks therefore have to consider what the impact of the attitudes they take towards the desirability of debt swap will be on their overall levels of prudence and the state of their balance sheet.

Foreign direct investment

In the 1960s foreign direct investment was the biggest source of private finance for the developing countries. The large multinational companies, particularly the American ones, scoured the world look-ing for suitable investment opportunities. In order to overcome tariff barriers and foreign exchange controls imposed by developing countries to try and keep American exports at bay the large multinational companies decided to set up domestic production in the developing countries themselves. The 1960s was the vintage decade of the great American household brand names. Ford car plants were built everywhere. Coca Cola and Pepsi toured the world to find suitable places to compete. Hoover and Kodak expanded in the richer countries. IBM expanded everywhere.

In the 1970s there was a fast acceleration in debt finance, partly at the expense of foreign direct equity investment. The attractions of debt finance to the host country were twofold. First, it meant there was a local name and local management put up over the asset purchased with the foreign money. Secondly, if the investment worked, it left the host country with more of the profits than under the direct foreign investment route. As we have seen, hope tri-umphed over experience and, in most cases, the country was left with a ruinously expensive debt to service and inadequately manag-ed assets to pay for it.

The OECD has charted the progress of direct investment flows from the OECD countries to the developing countries. The task is not easy. There are definitional problems over the distinction between a portfolio investment, where investors have a stake but not a controlling stake, and direct investment where investors usually have control. There is also a valuation problem, as the records are usually based on the original book cost whereas the cur-rent market value may be very different from that. The picture OECD paints is of a flow of investment fluctuating between prac-tically nothing in 1974 and almost £8 billion in the best years, 1975 and 1981. This is in sterling at 1970 value. In US dollars of the day, the 1981 peak reached a little over US$15 billion. Since then investment has been declining in both absolute and real terms.

If direct investment were to regain the level it was at in the late 1970s it could make a useful contribution to the gap created by the sharp decline in bank lending. Malaysia is one of the countries most successful in attracting direct foreign investment. It is running at the level of 3.5 per cent of its gross domestic product. As pointed out in an article in *The Economist* (June 1987), if Brazil could reach half the level that Malaysia enjoys it would gain an extra £3 billion a year which would account for almost half of its external financing needs.

The same pressures which are empowering the Japanese to become the principal lenders of money around the world, replacing the American banks, are also fuelling the expansion plans of the Japanese multinational companies. Where, in the 1960s, it was the American motor, computer and domestic products companies that were meeting resistance and problems in penetrating worldwide markets, it is now the Japanese motor, computer and chemical companies that are encountering that same resistance. All successful capitalist nations can become unpopular as their expansion encircles the world. It is one of the ironies of world economic history that the very companies and countries that do most to raise the general level of prosperity worldwide, by their successful exploitation of new processes and new products, are also the most likely targets for jealousy and political reprisals. The American multinationals and banks have often been the targets of socialist opposition in countries receiving them as investors. It is now the turn of the Japanese to experience the bitterness which economic success can spawn.

The Japanese strategy, like the American one before it, is most visible in establishing a strong bridgehead within the relatively affluent European community. Direct Japanese investment into the EEC, especially into the UK, is attempting to construct car, computer and household products factories in Europe itself, to reduce the pressure of exports from the Japanese mainland which arouse much greater political tensions. This strategy would definitely be followed up by more regular continent-hopping as the Japanese multinationals wish to maintain the momentum of their growth and need to find new markets to buy their products.

The Japanese motor and motorcycle industry is already very successful worldwide. The British and, to a lesser extent, the Italians have been in retreat for many years. They have been pulling back from their investments in developing countries. The Americans are not making the progress they used to achieve. It is now the turn of the Japanese car and motorcycle makers to become the dominant supplier worldwide, assembling or even making components in a variety of countries around the five continents. The same is true of the very successful Japanese domestic electronics companies and, as shown in Chapter 3, will be followed closely by the growing penetration of the Japanese banks.

The political arguments over direct foreign investment mirror those over debt swaps. Debt swap is a special form of encouraging direct foreign investment offering an added inducement to offset the political and economic risks of investing in a particular country. Direct foreign investment brings to the host country new skills, new products, new talents and better organisation. It brings a sum of money which might not otherwise be available for investment in the future and it links the remuneration of that capital investment to the results achieved.

Many countries, short of foreign exchange, are imposing controls either through debt swap or on direct forms of investment excluding debt swap. Through a control system they can, for example, specify that a given proportion of the output of any particular facility should earn hard currency foreign exchange by exporting the product. This enables the country to remunerate the capital in hard currency without depleting its foreign exchange reserves. Otherwise, a country heavily in debt and short of foreign exchange can find itself acting as host to a foreign investor wishing to service the domestic market. That foreign investor may do a very good job in supplying, for example, cars to the local marketplace, but all of this activity is in local currency. When the investor wants to take some profit or dividend to remunerate his own shareholders at home, the country can be faced with a foreign exchange problem. Import substitution or export potential are therefore often important criteria when a central bank comes to appraise a direct foreign investment project.

None the less, the countries which most successfully exploit direct inward investment are those with the greatest degree of political stability and the fewest controls. When a country has the confidence to dispense with controls foreign investors see this as a sign of strength and faith in local prospects. It was this, above all, which marked the transition of the UK government from retreat and defensiveness towards confidence and success. The abolition of foreign exchange controls by the Conservative government following the 1979 election victory was a bold step. At the time many commentators and all opposition politicians said that it would result in a major drain on the reserves and the controls would have to be re-imposed. The converse happened. Foreign investment poured into the UK and the pound sterling was bid up by the weight of money seeking to invest. It was a stark contrast to the experience in 1975–76, when an economy riddled with controls and tough foreign exchange rules experienced a flight of foreign money, reflecting the low level of confidence in the high borrowing, high spending policies then being pursued.

Direct foreign investment will have an important role to play in rebalancing the world economy. Those developing countries which are sensible enough to reduce controls and to welcome the foreign investor will be those that make most rapid progress to growth and higher prosperity. Economies like Singapore and Hong Kong have been based upon attracting a huge volume of footloose investment capital. The freedom of their markets and their climate of enterprise has enabled those two city states to build a prosperity out of all proportion to the real resource base of those barren rocks and peninsulas, and beyond the dreams of avarice of many of their neighbouring countries better endowed by nature. The lesson should be learned by those in developing countries: that a state has to allow its people to venture to prosper and has to be attractive to the investor.

Private project finance

Another means of bridging the financing gap which is growing in popularity is project finance. The financial technology for creating a free-standing project, into which a variety of investors can put their money, is developing rapidly. It is another one of those ideas, like privatisation, which is receiving a major stimulus from the richer part of the world as governments seek private financial solutions to what 10 or 20 years ago, would have been seen as public funding problems. But it is a technology which has often been deployed in the developing world, where there are huge opportunities for expansion.

The direct foreign investor described in the preceding section was seen largely in terms of the single multinational company wishing to build a branch plant or operating subsidiary in a new territory to exploit a wider market. Private project finance enables large multinational companies, or other investors, to club together to undertake a major project that is needed in a host economy. Alternatively, it is a way of financing a very large project which an individual multinational company could not afford on its own balance sheet. The project finance system enables the multinational company to act as project manager and part equity investor, usually keeping control of a project, whilst not having all of the financial strain upon its own balance sheet.

The most striking example of the new scale of project financing in Britain is the Channel Tunnel project. There have been experiments with privately financed tunnels before. The one that floundered in 1974 did so because a nationalised industry, British Rail, required massive public funding to make its contribution to the channel tunnel system. This money was not available in the restrained financial climate and so the Labour government cancelled the whole project. When the 1973/4 project was put together the ethos was still hostile to the whole idea of private risk in major public infrastructure projects. The climate has shifted markedly in the last two or three years.

Transport links are a prime example of important infrastructure projects that can add to the economic development of a large region or even that of a whole country. After World War II it was accepted that practically all transport links in most parts of the world would be supplied by government funding. The origins of modern transport, in the joint stock company boom of the railway era of Victorian Britain, or the toll based turnpikes of eighteenth century Europe, were forgotten. It was decided that transport links should be offered free, out of public money. This worked as long as governments had access to sufficient money to build enough facilities.

Once governments discovered they were doing too much and that they were becoming constrained by financial considerations it was natural that people would look again at the possibility of privately financing major transport projects. The Channel Tunnel was ideal, in many respects, for a privately financed project. It is very large in scale, and no government would be able to find several billions of pounds over a limited number of years to make the necessary investment. The revenue flows were clearly identifiable: trade and passenger movements across the channel are growing rapidly and most forecasters believe that they will continue to expand during the early years of the tunnel's life. The pricing was defined within fairly narrow parameters. It was already established that people should pay to get across the channel. All people currently making the journey pay to go on the hovercrafts or ferries or aeroplanes. There was, therefore, no political argument about the idea of imposing a toll on people making the journey. There was also some competitive check on the charge the new channel company could make, as it had to be related to the price of a ticket for a hovercraft.

To undertake financing of a large project it is usual to set up a separate company to run the project as a whole. The project normally has a defined life span, typically extending over a 25–50 year period. The equity base of the project might be quite small. The balance of the finance, once the equity has been raised, comes from long-term bank loans, pledged against security of the revenues the project is likely to earn over its life-span. The degree of equity needed and the level of interest charge built in depends on people's perceptions of the underlying risk of the project.

At one extreme the risk can be quite small. In the case of the Channel Tunnel the projectors have the guarantee of a monopoly of tunnel provision over the lifetime of their project when they need to remunerate their capital. This cuts the risks quite considerably. Three basic risks are assumed by the projectors. First there is the risk that the original estimates of capital cost will prove far too low. Unforeseen geological problems, disasters with the tunnelling equipment, simple miscalculations of inflation rates or the difficulty of assembling various kind of structures could lead to a substantial overrun, thereby making it much more difficult to remunerate the capital.

Secondly there is the possibility that traffic growth will prove disappointing. If the EEC economies went into a major recession during the early years after the tunnel opening, or if some unforeseen competitor developed, more price-efficient at getting across the channel, then the projections of revenues could be greatly upset. Thirdly, there is the possibility that the main losers from the tunnel project, the ferry and hovercraft operators, could find a way to damage the tunnel in its early years, even at the expense of their own revenues, by going for market share. This too could have a damaging impact upon the remuneration of the project, as all projects are very sensitive to the revenues received in the first few years after their completion.

At the other extreme project-financing underwrites activities that have a much greater degree of risk. The traditional origins of the project financing system lie in mineral workings. A natural resource project has a finite span of life based on the reserves of the particular resource. Consider, for example, a gold mine which is expected to sustain 25 years of production. The project financier has to take into account a variety of high risk factors.

First there is the question of political risk in the country in which he is investing. Because a very high proportion of gold is mined and exported from South Africa there is always the danger that the vagaries of South African politics might affect the gold market. Leaving that aside the project financier has to consider the individual risk in the country in which his mine is going to be sunk. Gold mines can attract the greedy depredations of host country governments. They may fall short of complete nationalisation at some date in the future, but, after the mine is up and running, they may decide to impose new rules concerning the export of gold or the remittance of dividends or profits.

Then, the project financier has to consider the great fluctuations in the price of the metal. In the last 20 years the gold price has fluctuated between US $35 an ounce and US $700 an ounce. Its future price course is uncertain. The mine may be extremely profitable at US $500 an ounce and unprofitable at US $250 an ounce. Starting from the current price position the financier has to make his best estimates of what is likely to happen to the gold price over the life of the mine. If he is prudent, he will also work out how robust the project would be in a time of declining gold prices and he will examine the cash and profit flows very carefully to see just how low a gold price he can accept before his project ceases to be profitable.

Thirdly, the financier has to consider the competence and the commitment of the gold mining company or companies involved in the project. Is the mine likely to live up to expectations? Will the reserves last for 25 years as estimated? Could there be unforeseen geological problems half-way through the vein which could deplete the reserves or make mining much more expensive? Is the mine workforce likely to co-operate or will the wages spiral out of control, cutting the attractiveness of the operation? Can the machinery be acquired and delivered on time and will it work?

The project finance team has to piece together all these different risk factors and construct a series of cash flows. In the early years of any project, whether it's a mine or an infrastructure project, all of the money will be going out. Each major project has a period of one to six or seven years when it is all spend and no return. The very essence of project financing is to raise money to make huge investments which have to be repaid over a long timespan.

Once the basic cash flows have been constructed the project financier will vary crucial assumptions to see what happens if things go wrong. The usual analytical technique is to discount a stream of future cash flows. Having constructed year-by-year or month-by-month the revenues coming in and the costs going out an annual discount rate will then be applied to all those monies so that the total proceeds of the project to the initial investor can be expressed as a single figure called the net present value. A comparison of net present values against the risk factors, and a comparison between projects, is then possible. The investor putting in the equity will be looking for a substantial return reflecting the very high risk of his investment. The bankers contemplating advancing the loan capital to support the bulk of the project will be looking at how much protection there is for their interest charges in the forecasted cash flows. The host country will be looking at whether the returns are just or unreasonable and what they can do by way of imposing taxes or regulations on the project without stifling it at birth. A complicated series of negotiations ensues between sponsoring banks, lead investors, host government and the mining or project managing companies. Sometimes, because of the risk of the project, the managing companies will seek remuneration by way of a fee or royalty on the revenues rather than seeking themselves to become heavy equity investors taking their profits out through their shareholdings. This then entails even more detailed analysis on behalf of the actual equity investors who will be shouldering the bulk of the risk.

The expansion of mining and natural resource project finance technology into a whole host of new areas has become possible because governments are having to relinquish their grip on so many traditional public sector areas. In Turkey a build, operate and transfer project is underway for a thermal power plant. This will entail a US $100 million inward investment into the country.

Under a build, operate and transfer competition a host government, which would previously have undertaken an investment in the public sector, puts out to international tender the given infrastructure project. A good tender document sets out precisely the rules under which the contractor will operate. In this case the contractors were asked to build the thermal power station and to operate for a period of years during which time they could themselves withdraw their profits. They are to transfer the resulting facility, once it had been fully paid for, at the end of a specified period, free of charge, to the government of Turkey.

Handing over the asset free of charge at the end of a specified period is not as big an obstacle as some might think in the minds of those seeking to do the work. Given that projects are evaluated on a discounted cash flow basis, the revenues coming into the project after 20 or 30 years have practically no value when it comes to making an assessment today of how to reward the project. The time horizon of many investors is still quite short. Because of the political, technical and market risks that they are incurring, they wish to see their capital repaid and their profits achieved within a reasonable period of years. No one can forecast all the variables involved in something like a thermal power plant 25 or 30 years into the future with any degree of accuracy. In consequence no one of any sense puts much value on the asset at the end of the period and its free transfer to the state is a considerable bonus for the government of Turkey but of no great business relevance.

What matters much more to the potential investor is his assessment of the political and economic risks in the early years of the contract and the willingness of the government to allow a reasonable amount of money to be spent on retiring the loans and remunerating the equity holders in those early years. Build, operate and transfer projects are likely to figure prominently in the next five years. They are a development from the turn key contract, where a contractor in the lead on a project would put together a team to design, build and bring on stream a major plant which was then handed over to the host government in return for the capital value. The turn key project is no longer feasible in many parts of the world because of the difficulties the governments have in paying for it.

The scale of projects worldwide is still large. China has recently been negotiating for a US $3.7 billion nuclear power plant. In Egypt another US $3 billion is being spent in 1987 on power plants, in Libya US $3.3 billion worth of irrigation is required, in Morocco a US $150 million airport expansion, in Iran a US $150 million railway, in Nigeria a US $550 million oil refinery and a US $600 million ethylene plant, in South Korea US $3billion worth of nuclear powerplant equipment, in Sri Lanka a US $483 million hydro plant, in Taiwan a US $5 billion mass transit system and in Turkey a US $295 million motorway. This is just a selection from a large and expanding marketplace.

The most common items are natural resource, public utility and transportation projects. Current lines of thought on electricity privatisation in the United Kingdom are having considerable influence on how the financing of electricity projects is viewed worldwide. The experiment in the United Kingdom with the Northern Ireland lignite power station is an important pioneering piece of work. The idea is that the Northern Ireland lignite station will have a defined contract to sell electricity into the nationalised grid system. This contract will specify volumes and control prices. The contract then becomes a proposition. The government is seeking private finance to design, build and operate the lignite power station. The project financiers are discovering that the contract to sell power is of bankable value.

This technique can be applied widely to the modernisation and expansion of electricity systems. Electricity is particularly favoured as the large lumpy investments in individual power stations represent sensible units of investment for major project financing. But it is also possible to contemplate major project financings in the oil, gas, water and transport industries. Mass transit systems have a clear revenue stream which is predictable within certain markets. They have a monopoly element over a certain kind of transport provision, but have to compete against private motorcars, walking, cycling and other cross-city travel systems. Pipeline systems for oil and gas, subject to price regulation, can also be suitable cases for project finance treatment. Oil refineries and petrochemical works, large capital projects, may also attract project financing as well as direct investment by the large multinational oil and chemical companies worldwide.

The risks in project financing are obvious. As with direct inward investment there is always the threat of political change encouraging nationalisation with or without compensation or a change in the rules concerning the repatriation of profit and dividend. The advantages are also clear. The structure of a project finance enables the investment to be properly managed by companies that know what they are doing without too much government intervention in the day-to-day detail. The initial private finance negotiations establish ground rules which may survive long enough to enable the project team and investors to remunerate themselves. The system enables host countries to build modern facilities on a large scale which they could not otherwise afford and which their domestic companies would not be able to establish or manage adequately. Project financing is another part of the new financial technology which will fill the gap created by the collapse of government confidence and government resources in the process of development itself.

The new financial technology draws heavily on methods and systems that pre-date the great boom in bank lending of the 1970s. The novelty lies in the need to retire debt from over-extended banks and to inject new urgency and variety into the forms of equity finance in the developing world.

The great shift in the thrust of inward investment to developing countries is coming from the Japanese surplus and the American deficit. The new wave of Japanese investors are still largely financing themselves through borrowings from Japanese banks. To this will be added a growing volume of re-invested profits as multi-nationals expand abroad and a growing volume of equity investment as debt swap, privatisation and, more especially, project finance, comes to make its mark.

All of these techniques point in the direction of a much larger volume of equity funding and a much lower volume of debt funding. The world has become over-geared and is desperately trying to adjust the balance. A necessary precondition for success will be the rapid growth of markets capable of trading equity securities. There is not necessarily a shortage of savings worldwide. There is instead a caution which means that many savers in Third World countries invest in American bonds, stamp collections, art or other unproductive activities. That same caution means that many developed countries invest their savings domestically or through their banking systems rather than in direct equity stakes in the developing world where the opportunities are greater but the risks higher.

The next part of the story is to demonstrate how the world's equity markets themselves are going through a major metamorphosis. There are signs that in stock markets from London to Auckland and most places between, dramatic change is now under way. The volume of stock being traded is leaping upwards and the styles of market activity are adjusting to the new accent on equity. The 1990s will be the decade of the international equity. The 1980s are slowly piecing together the mechanisms that will make that possible, a process which not even the October 1987 crash and a bear market can prevent.

6

Making a Market: The Growth of International Stock Exchanges

One of the important developments in enterprise capitalism was the growth of stock markets. Before the advent of traded transfers of securities it was difficult for entrepreneurs to tap the savings of the towns and countryside of a developing country. Lack of knowledge and information about who was saving on the part of the entrepreneur, combined with a suspicion or lack of knowledge on the part of the potential investor, meant that capital was saved in less productive ways and business growth was constrained by the difficulty of obtaining money. The growth of enterprise capitalism was therefore usually linked to the development of a banking system. Banks acted as the intermediaries, taking in deposits from those with savings and making advances to those with business ideas.

But business, as we have seen, also needs equity investment. Not all of it could come from people who had already made savings and then had good business ideas which they were prepared to back with their own money. Not all of the businesses could grow patiently and smoothly, reinvesting the profits to meet all of their capital requirements. So, at different times, countries developed different methods of intermediating between savers and investors. Very often a strong family-based business culture developed. In the late seventeenth and early eighteenth centuries in the UK lawyers and other responsible people in the community started to introduce people with savings to those with business ideas. This is a method which can still be seen in developing countries, along with the extended family coming to the aid of the enterprising young man.

The development of the stock exchange can take a country's growth onto a different level. In the UK stock exchange trading began in London quite early on. Businessmen and intermediaries got together in the coffeehouses of the City and started to make out pieces of paper representing share stakes in companies. The explosive growth of the joint stock company as a vehicle for Victorian enterprise capitalism showed how powerful a mechanism this was.

The joint stock company was adopted around the world. It was a way of dissociating ownership from management. It gave the providers of the capital the ultimate right to change the management, to intervene in policy, to vote on all matters of major importance. It gave to the managers the right, in normal circumstances, to run the business as long as they remunerated the capital and made adequate reports of what they were doing to the annual general meeting.

Savers do not like illiquid forms of investment. If you invest in your neighbour's company, he does not want you removing your capital two years later if your circumstances have changed, or if you change your mind about the prospects for his business. The role of the coffeehouse marketmakers was to guarantee to an individual that he could, at a price, sell his investment whenever he wished. The London-based coffeehouse market was soon replaced by a more formal structure and, in the heyday of Victorian capitalism, regional stock exchanges mushroomed across Britain from Bristol to Manchester, from London to Scotland. Each of these regional markets acted as a means of bringing the local savings of the community into the use of local entrepreneurs.

Britain was not unique in developing a strong equity-based capital market. American capitalism exploded on the back of a series of regional exchanges across that large continent, with New York soon establishing its dominance as the principal financial centre serving the whole nation. In Europe, Paris, Brussels, Milan, Madrid and other capitals also developed some kind of equity-based trading market. Often this was a small, under-resourced supplement to the principal financial market in a capital city, the market in government debt which raised money for public purposes.

In the 1970s, the epoch of massive bank lending around the world, the cult of the equity was in retreat. It had had a good period in the post-war boom, paralleling the rise of the large American multinational companies and the explosion of consumer-based activity as new products were brought to a mass market. The 1970s was something different. It was a period of economic restriction as the logic of over-borrowing came to bear down heavily on world economies and as the fact of higher oil and commodity prices worked its way through to activity.

In London the primary equity market of the 1970s almost ground to a halt. The main task facing the London stock market was to provide billions of pounds each year for government purposes through supporting endless issues of government bonds. In New York the equity market continued to provide substantial sums of money for business purposes but the indices were stuck in a narrow trading range and, for years, investors made mediocre returns, reflecting the underlying pressures on profitability and the impact of inflation on all types of business. European equity markets did very little. Many of the large companies in each of the countries concerned were either subsidiaries of foreign multinationals whose shares traded on Wall Street and nowhere else, or they were large family-backed companies in private ownership where owners thought it not worthwhile obtaining a quotation. The bourses of Europe were underdeveloped and unimportant in the provision of new capital for business growth.

The rise of Tokyo as a major international stock exchange was a central feature of the 1970s and early 1980s. The Tokyo market provided a strong underlying market in the equity of Japanese companies. It was primarily a domestic marketplace, but one which became increasingly attractive to investors from overseas as they saw the strength of the Japanese miracle and wished to participate directly in the productivity and production successes of the Japanese enterprise culture. The strength of the yen was an added inducement to overseas investors to seek out Japanese equity opportunities.

During the 1970s the big three stock markets of the world, New York, London and Tokyo, remained fairly insular. It is true that international investing funds, particularly those based in London, looked for more and more opportunities to invest overseas. Their two ports of call were always the US and Japan. It is also true that a few companies began to explore the possibilities of having a New York quote if they were London based or of having a London quote if they were American based, but this was the exception rather than the rule. Whilst the debt markets were busily constructing a large international chain of transactions and enjoying the benefits of syndication of loans and bond trading, the equity markets remained small in scale and narrowly nationalistic.

This separation of markets was encouraged and underwritten by very different practices. The US market went for deregulation earlier than the London market. The New York market is based on a series of specialist traders who make a market in shares. The deregulation of broking houses led to a large reduction in commissions and a substantial increase in volumes traded. It had to be backed up by intensification of regulation under the Stock Exchange Commission which set out clear rules governing the listing of new equities, the trading of existing equities and the conduct of market practitioners.

In London the broking cartel survived until the mid-1980s. London enforced a complete split between market making, which was carried out by a limited number of jobbing firms, on the one hand and brokers who acted as agents for clients on the other. A UK share purchaser had to deal through the intermediary, a stockbroker, who charged a fixed commission specified in nationally agreed broking commission rates. The broker in turn would deal with a jobber who would remunerate himself by the difference between the offer and bid prices, his buying and selling prices. The result of retaining two separate functions and having an agreed commission structure was that a typical transaction in London could cost around 5 per cent. On top of this the government imposed a 2 per cent stamp duty payable by the purchaser of the shares. London was therefore an expensive market in which to deal. When coupled with foreign exchange controls and other government interventions in the 1970s it meant that London was an unattractive place in which to have shares quoted.

The role of technology in transforming equity markets should not be underestimated. Trading until the mid-1980s took place in single physical locations at specified times. The whole system was based upon a deal between the marketmaker and the broker. They looked at each other eyeball to eyeball and struck their bargain in person. It was later confirmed by means of a written contract and the whole system rested on trust between jobber and broker and upon their separate jotting down of the transaction they had undertaken.

The advent of high-powered computing meant that it was possible to carry out a bargain between computer screens. Someone wishing to buy a share could, theoretically, tap in on his keyboard the share he wished to buy and see the range of market quotes. He could then tap back a message to the marketmaker making the offer he liked best, make a phone call, place his bargain and have it confirmed through the computer system.

In the mid-1980s pressures of technology combined with the pressures of deregulatory politics to bring a fundamental change to the London stock markets. The idea that stockbroking commission rates could be the subject of cartel practices, and that the competition between stockbrokers should be limited to competition over quality of research and recommendations was under political attack by the early 1980s. If monopoly trade unions were to be subjected to fundamental changes to break their stranglehold on whole industries, and if public monopoly enterprises were to see their monopolies questioned, was it not time, the commentators rightly asked, for some of the professional monopolies to be explored and reformed as well? The most obvious monopoly to attack was the Stock Market, where dealing rates were high, where international practice was beginning to move away from the London system, and where the high levels of income made them a natural source of envy.

As a result the London Stock Market was referred to the Office of Fair Trading to examine the cartel. The Secretary of State for Trade and Industry Cecil Parkinson inherited this situation and made a brave decision. He decided to cancel the OFT enquiries into the Stock Exchange if, in return, the Stock Exchange would carry out its own reforms. The commission cartel had to be removed.

The Stock Exchange agreed. Many of those who made the decision to take this course were of the original opinion that the changes they would have to undertake would be limited and that they had struck a good bargain. As the months went by it was clear that the twin pressures of competitive business interests and new technology were going to transform the London Stock Market out of all recognition.

It soon became obvious that London was going to scrap the distinction between broker and jobber. It opted for a united system more like the American one, where marketmaking could be carried out by anyone with sufficient capital and skill. Some would try and survive as agency brokers but the power was going to shift to those who could offer a complete service to the client. Commissions were going to be cut substantially, particularly on the large bargains. In many cases the commission would go altogether, leaving the marketmaker with the difference between the bid and the offer price. Much more capacity was going to come into the market. One of the constraints on the expansion of the Stock Market was the inadequacy of the capital of the jobbing firms. This limited the amount of stock they could purchase and run on their books, and therefore limited the size of the market they could make in any given security. The advent of freer marketmaking meant that large new concerns were going to be created, or would arrive in the London market, which could then use their financial muscle power to hold securities and make markets in them.

When the new Stock Market first started to trade many felt the action would still take place primarily on the fixed trading floor of the Stock Exchange tower building. The new building of the London Stock Exchange had only been in use since the early 1970s. Yet, within a few weeks of the 'Big Bang' deregulation, the Stock Exchange was empty. Brokers turned with alacrity to carrying out transactions through television screens linked to computers. The market ceased to exist in a physical sense. It came to reside in a series of wires linking marketmakers' offices and broking offices around the City.

An individual wishing to carry out a transaction could, at the press of a button, see all the available quotes in the market. At the press of another buttom and a short phone call he could have bought or sold substantial quantities of shares and his transaction would then appear on the screen as another movement in the market.

This kind of technology not only reduced the time it took to carry out a bargain and cut the cost of executing one but opened the door to much more cross-border trading between countries. If it is possible to trade with anyone in England at the press of a computer button, by a simple extension on the international phone lines it is possible to trade with similar speed and facility in New York, Tokyo or a host of other centres around the world. It was a question of who was going to be technically sophisticated and open enough to link their machinery to the growing international machinery of dealing.

When the first, strongest links were forged between London and New York, many of the New York financial institutions took a prominent role in refashioning the British city. British broking firms proved alert to the opportunities and were often happy to sell themselves out or amalgamate their activities with larger American financial conglomerates. The Japanese, too, were keen to gain a position in the UK as financial operators and marketmakers. They forged alliances and developed their own businesses. As the City reshaped itself and equipped itself for the modern age, so its trading links with Tokyo and with New York were strengthened.

The government had meanwhile cut stamp duty on new share purchases from 2 per cent to ½ per cent and all of the complicated structure of exchange controls had been demolished at the end of the 1970s. London was now poised at the middle of the time zones and at the centre of the English-speaking world to take substantial business. The business started to roll in. Many US companies decided it was worthwhile having a London quote as their foothold in the European financial world. More London companies decided that they needed to be able to raise equity simultaneously in New York and Tokyo, as well as in London, and started to arrange the necessary quotations. But above all it was government activity which led the way in pioneering the simultaneous issue of shares in many markets around the world, as part of the privatisation bonanza.

The crucial share issue which changed the face of equity issues in London and, to a great extent, around the world, was the massive offer for sale of ordinary shares in British Telecom. By 28 November 1984 the government planned to sell just over 3000 million ordinary shares in British Telecom at £1.30 each. This £4000 million offering was the largest ever, by a long way, in the London market, and the largest ever attempted worldwide. By modern standards the scale seems only moderately large. At the time it was undertaken it was massive and it was the perception of its size which led to many of the issue's innovations.

Only a year earlier there were many financial experts who thought that a share offering on this scale would never succeed. They had played around with many ways of avoiding an issue of this size. Some said that British Telecom could not be privatised at all. Some said it could not be privatised in one go. A series of tranches should be spread out over a number of years in order to allow the market to accommodate the volume of shares being sold. Some wished to see a substantial part of the British Telecom capital sold as bonds, as everybody agreed the sale of £2–£3 billion of bonds was quite possible as governments worldwide had shown in their massive offering of public debt. The government was, none the less, resolved to sell the company as an equity concern and to put at least 51 per cent into a single offering even though this entailed raising some £4000 million (*British Telecom Prospectus*, Nov. 1984).

The planning of the issue led the government and its closest advisers to the conclusion that the confines of the normal equity market must be expanded dramatically in order to absorb the volume of shares. A tripartite strategy was hit upon. The issue would attempt to attract substantial funds from the normal source of investment in UK equities, the institutional market. The 1970s and early 1980s had seen a further sharp movement in the direction of all new equity investment taking place through the intermediation of pension funds and life insurance companies. For years the small investor in the UK, the successor to the Victorian enterprise capitalist using his regional stock exchange, had been on the retreat and had been selling. The institutions not only had to pay for any new issues, or extra capital issues being made by existing companies, but they also had to buy substantial amounts of shares being sold regularly by the community of small investors. It was those who thought that the Stock Exchange would always rest upon institutional appetite for equity investment who felt that the British Telecom issue could not be done, or who predicted that it was too large.

The second target market for British Telecom lay overseas. Elaborate plans were undertaken to have a simultaneous issue in the USA, Canada, Japan and continental Europe. The government appointed Morgan Stanley and Company in the US, McLeod Young Weir in Canada, Nomura Securities in Japan and Swiss Bank Corporation in continental Europe to sell almost 15 per cent of the Group. The Bank of England itself underwrote these shares in case there was inadequate international demand. By this means the domestic investors knew that a substantial portion of the equity was not going to be available for their purchases.

The third part of the strategy was to encourage a whole new army of small shareholders to come into the UK market to buy a share for the first time. This army could be mustered from three sources. First it was decided to target the British Telecom employees. A special offering was worked out, based on the grant of some free shares, the grant of matching shares for those purchased, and a priority allocation system for those purchased at full price. The second target market was British Telecom's huge subscriber network. Every subscriber was sent information on the share sale and was advised of the opportunity to obtain a reduction on subsequent telephone bills related to the number of shares purchased. The third target was the wider public which required a retail marketing plan on a scale never before seen in British equity offerings.

Building a large retail market for an offer the size of British Telecom was exciting work. Basic information about British Telecom had to be prepared and distributed to as large a number of people as possible. This necessitated a vast printing job to make sure that the prospectus, the basic document setting out information about British Telecom, was widely circulated. Supporting documentation was also produced giving background on British Telecom in a form accessible to the lay reader.

It was also necessary to explain to the new generation of potential share buyers the nature of share ownership. With this in mind share information offices were set up which handled the queries of individuals contemplating equity investment. For example, a common query was how an investor could sell his shares again. The information office had to explain the use of stockbrokers or banks and the function of the market in giving him value for his equity.

The need to raise public awareness of what was going on was facilitated by the natural press interest in a large political and economic event. The opponents of the privatisation had done a great deal to make the public aware of it. The unions had opposed it tooth and nail and the Labour opposition had raised it during the preceding general election campaign. The prospectus itself had to contain a warning concerning the attitude of the opposition party, for in its 1983 manifesto the Labour Party stated 'it would return to public ownership the public assets and rights hived off by the Tories, with compensation of no more than that received when the assets were denationalised'. Labour was threatening to buy back the shares of anyone purchasing them at the same price they had paid for them. As this was an event that could not take place for another three years it meant that, if it had been implemented, the individual purchasers would have lost all the interest their savings could otherwise have earned. The presence of this threat did deter some, but it was another factor making the whole process newsworthy. The vendors of British Telecom backed up the natural news interest in the issue with a huge public advertising campaign. Television was brought in to orchestrate a powerful media blitz around the theme of British Telecom, the power beind the button. Market research surveys indicated that people viewed British Telecom as a stodgy public utility. The advertising agency decided to project an image of British Telecom as a company at the cutting edge of high technology, with good growth prospects because of the natural growth of communications business worldwide and the impact that the new technology would have on lifestyles and patterns of telecommunication usage.

The combined impact of editorial coverage of the big event, a well orchestrated public advertising campaign, the groundwork carried out by the share information offices and the press explaining the advantages and disadvantages of share ownership, ensured massive public interest in the issue.

A few months before the issue was to hit the streets the institutional investors were still playing hard to get. They were telling the government and its advisers at every conceivable opportunity that the issue was too large, that British Telecom was an unexciting company, and that therefore the price of the shares had to be low if the issue was to have any chance of success. This pressure continued right up to the pricing day. The advisers were naturally cautious, deeply immersed in the City culture and afraid that the issue could be a flop. The small investor demand was still uncertain. People were aware that a large number of people knew about the issue and had expressed interest in it but no one could be sure how much of this interest would convert into direct sales.

The structure of the issue had, of course, reduced as many of the risks as possible. Because the issue was so large it was likely to place a substantial strain on the banking and monetary system of the country. To help compensate for this, and to reduce the impact on the cash available for stock market investment, in the first instance it was decided that British Telecom should be sold in partly paid form. Fifty pence per share out of the total £1.30 was payable in late November 1984 at the time of the applications. A further 40 pence per share was payable on 24 June 1985 and the final 40 pence was not payable until 9 April 1986. In this way the proceeds of the sale were split roughly into thirds and were spread over three separate government financial years, giving the Treasury much needed capital receipts for three separate budgets. The decision to sell over 400,000 shares abroad also lifted the cash pressures on the London market. The decision to price the shares at £1.30 also meant that they were a very attractive offer. On the offer for sale basis, the shares were providing a running yield of more than 7 per cent. The price earnings ratio was under ten times, below the market average.

This decision was understandable. British Telecom's profits, although capable of growth through improved efficiency, would be constrained by the total rate of growth of the British economy. Whilst volume growth would be strong because of the general trend to telecommunications growth in a buoyant economy, profits would suffer in part from the new price control, which had been built into the regulatory formula. As a result the judgment was made that the sale of the issue, coupled with the moderate outlook for the company, required a discount to the Stock Market as a whole.

This pricing decision made inevitable a runaway success of British Telecom. All those involved in the final pricing decision doubtless believed they came to the right answer. Had they chosen a higher price, they could easily have put off the army of small investors, without whom the issue would have flopped.

The applications poured in. The issue was heavily oversubscribed and in early trading the shares went to a 30 per cent premium.

The world's largest equity offering had been a runaway success and the accusations followed, not that it had been a disaster, but that the shares had been sold too cheaply.

British Telecom brought 2.5 million shareholders into the UK market, 1 million of whom had never owned shares before. It was a triumphant display of popular capitalism in action. A stock market which had atrophied under the combined pressures of an endless diet of government debt issues and the growing institutionalisation of savings had made a massive breakout in two directions at the same time. British Telecom changed the balance between equity and government bond issues on its own, because of the scale. It was also the first sign that the trend towards fewer and fewer private investors could be decisively reversed.

The techniques pioneered in the British Telecom sale have now become commonplace in large scale world equity offerings. The Japanese copied it for their massive sale of Nippon Telephone and Telegraph. The French copied it for their large privatisation sales. The British themselves have copied and developed it in the British Gas and British Petroleum offers which have since far exceeded British Telecom in their scale and ambition. But in each case the essence of the idea remains the same — to expand the domestic equity market by attracting new shareholders, to put pressure on the institutions by creating a shortage of stock, and to take the pressure off the domestic market by a large simultaneous international offering.

The growth of a retail market for stocks and shares developed further and faster in the US than anywhere else. When Britain was experiencing painful contraction in its private shareholding, America sustained and developed it. As a result a different market infrastructure developed. In America the connection between retailing and share sales was understood. You can go into a share shop in America and buy shares in your lunch break over the counter. No such facility existed in the UK as there was insufficient volume of business from the private investor. Regional brokers also survived much longer in the US because there was local business to be had. They also developed more quickly the knack of operating on two levels, providing a local focus for market activity and exploiting the range of markets, especially in New York, to carry out some of their transactions.

In order to handle a sale the size of British Telecom it was necessary to develop adequate dealing arrangements. For the first two years after the share sale regional co-ordinators were organised to enable people to deal locally in British Telecom shares at reduced rates of commission. For sale transactions less than £300 the commission was limited to £5 only, and on bargains up to £424 to £7. It was possible to buy up to £606 with a commission limited to £10. Regional co-ordinators were established in London, Aberdeen, Belfast, Birmingham, Bristol, Cardiff, Edinburgh, Glasgow, Lincoln, Liverpool, Manchester, Middlesborough, Newcastle-upon-Tyne, Plymouth, Reading and the South East. This was, in embryo, a revival of the old provincial stock exchanges, linked to London and capable of dealing with substantial retail demand. It was also a harbinger of low commission rates, which would become a matter of course for the large investor a few months later with the Big Bang deregulation.

On the back of this new interest in the retail market, brokers began cautiously to experiment with retail establishments themselves. High Street stores were at the same time looking for ways to diversify into higher value products and were beginning to understand the possibilities of financial retailing, including pension plans, life insurance and, conceivably, share sales.

The move towards a proper retail market was greatly facilitated by changes under way in the bank and building society world. The banks and building societies had been at war with each other for several years. The building societies argued that the banks were given tax advantages and had a natural advantage, through their control of the cheque clearing system, in aggregating savings and using them for a variety of business purposes. The banks argued that, because the building societies paid a composite rate of tax on their deposits, they were getting a tax benefit which enabled them to have a dominant position in the mortgage market.

Originally the building societies were friendly societies for accumulating savings, offering people a relatively secure haven and a reasonable interest rate, and lending the money to a multitude of borrowers who wished to purchase their own home. All of the money was secured against domestic property. In the UK this was a fairly reliable security as, on the whole, house prices tended to rise or remain stable, rather than fall.

Technology and deregulation were again the driving forces behind reconsideration of the relatively stable, if acrimonious, position between bank and building society. The result of the rethink of policy over the building societies' legislation, and the tax changes, was to allow a much greater degree of convergence. Whilst building societies are still primarily limited to dealing in mortgages, they are now allowed to use a portion of their assets for other kinds of lending and to support other types of financial service activity. The banks, meanwhile, have counter-attacked by making a major entry into the mortgage market. They too wish to diversify from simply being involved in the accumulation of deposits and lending to individuals and companies. They have come to see the powerful place their branch network can hold in developing a retail financial services network. There are signs, early in 1988, that building societies themselves will seek a quotation and raise new money through share issues.

In the early years around the time of the British Telecom issue, banks, building societies and high street shops were still very cautious. There was considerable scepticism about whether the British public would ever, like the American, want to come in off the streets and buy and sell shares. There was caution about retailing ordinary financial products. It was accepted that unit trusts, unit linked insurance and life insurance were more likely to be sold as they always had been, through telephone selling and mail order.

Changes of regulations in the tax regime precipitated more interest in share and financial product selling through bank and building society branches. This was reinforced by another important government policy initiative. One of the main reasons for institutional domination in the savings marketplace in the UK was the strong growth of pensions as the most attractive form of saving, and the acceptance by all concerned that pensions had to be invested by professionals through large, company-based pension funds. The only thing that could in any way compare with the complete tax break offered on the investment in the pension fund, on the income and capital gain made by the fund and on the lump sum paid on retirement, was the modest tax relief afforded to individuals taking out life insurance. When the Conservative government abolished the tax relief on life insurance premiums the life insurance market had to rethink its strategy and reorient its marketing, selling to people the idea of the intrinsic worth of having an equity stake in the commercial and industrial life of the country. Previously, they had been able to sell the whole idea of life insurance-based investment on the strength of a good tax break.

The government was faced with a dilemma when it came to review the reasons for institutional dominance in the savings market, and face the irreducible fact that it all rested upon complete tax relief for pensions which was, in its turn, extremely popular. Rather than create enormous political difficulties for itself by threatening the tax relief, it was decided instead to offer similar attractions to individuals who wished to set up their own pensions savings scheme.

There was a clear precedent in that the self-employed were already allowed to set up their own individual pension funds and gain tax relief for so doing. The rules governing the tax relief on these schemes were not as generous as those concerning major company schemes, but they did represent far and away the most tax efficient way of saving for the self-employed. They were very popular with the self-employed within the two decades prior to their retirement, and the provisions allowing some accelerated funding in those years were often used to the full.

The advent of personal portable pensions was a major breakthrough for those who wished to see a broader spread of wealth throughout the community and a direct connection between individual ownership and the commercial life of the nation. Eleven million people own shares indirectly through the intermediation of their company pension fund. A large number of those might prefer to have their own personal pension fund, so that their assets are not destroyed when they change job and so that they can have control over who advises or runs the investments. The possible growth of personal portable pensions, especially suited to the new footloose industries and the footloose career styles of many executives, lies behind the thinking of some retailers, banks and building societies now interested in building a financial services business.

The development of high-tech international financial trading has brought with it a substantial number of legal and regulatory problems. Different laws and different standards apply in the different markets of the world. Where countries like the US and the UK have made insider trading an offence, in other countries, like New Zealand, it is still legal. How could the administrations, which were national, police and handle a situation where different standards applied and where share dealers and traders could hop across boundaries on their computers, choosing where they wished to undertake a deal and how they wished to take their profits? In the age of the train and the face-to-face deal things took a little longer and money often had to be physically moved, in suitcases, across borders, to be delivered safely into the hands of banks which did not ask too many questions. Now it was possible, through a complex series of computer transactions, to cover the traces of illicit dealing more rapidly.

How too could the authorities be sure that markets were not being taken advantage of in other ways? It has always been accepted that there needs to be a clear series of rules governing the listing of a new security on the stock market. The authorities have to satisfy themselves that the company is sensibly run, has established a track record, keeps adequate books of account and is likely to make honest reports to its stockholders. In the wave of new listings which growing enterprise unleashed, it became even more important to make sure that these niceties were being observed. In a fast changing international world companies could be careful about which authority they chose as the listing agency. Could the world reach the point where a great deal of 'flagging out' would occur, as companies sought to migrate from the heavily regulated areas to the lightly policed growing markets? Could people also be sure that, in this new footloose world, with a large number of new marketmakers in London and fairly open entry in New York, that they would receive their share certificates on time or they would get due value for the shares they had sold?

In London a great deal of thought was put into the question of how the financial services industries could best be regulated. In January 1985 the government issued a White Paper entitled 'Financial Services in the United Kingdom: a new framework for investor protection'. This document set out the difficulties. First, a satisfactory definition of 'investment' had to be determined, to include all the new types of tradable security that were being pioneered. It had to include futures and options as well as ordinary equities, bonds, convertibles and a range of other hybrid securities. An investment business had to be defined, for the investment businesses had themselves to be brought under some kind of regulatory supervision. Authority had to be established in the hands of the government and of the regulatory bodies to make sure that those coming under their guidance understood that the regulations were to be enforced and that ultimately the powers were there to take the necessary disciplinary action.

In the debate that followed there were two broad currents of thought. One group saw that the market was going to be protean. It was developing so rapidly, and technology and techniques were changing so swiftly, that it would be impossible for regulatory authorities to foresee all the permutations and changes. It was therefore necessary to set out a simple and clear framework of law. If a business failed to give value for shares sold on time, if there was inadequate separation of client accounts and the business's own accounts, if money or shares went missing, if there was inadequate control and reporting on investment portfolios under management, if information was used to trade against the insider trader regulations, and if the business was conducted in the best interests of the business rather than its clients, then it had to be accepted that legal offences had been committed. The individuals responsible should be brought before the courts to stand charge, usually on something that amounts to simple theft.

The alternative view was that financial dealings were so complicated that there should be a separate series of regulations. These could often be best guided by a committee or grouping of practitioners together with lay people. This body would set out in advance what the rules were, and they would regulate the industry accordingly. This faction split in two. Some wished to see the rules given the force of statute law and run directly by the government. Others wished to see the groups of lay people and practitioners turned into self-regulatory bodies with disciplinary powers only referring very severe cases to the Public Prosecutor.

Many felt that adopting the Securities and Exchange Commission idea from the States was undesirable. Most American commentators felt that it was too cumbersome and complicated, a constraint on the development of the American financial services industry. None the less, there was a natural tendency in Parliament and government circles to seek a solution which gave ultimate power to the state and to infer from this that the state had to be involved in a great deal of detailed regulation and control.

The resulting UK system is a hybrid. It has ultimate statutory backing from the Financial Services Act. It has a self-regulatory body with considerable disciplinary powers drawing on the wisdom of both practitioners and lay people. There is plenty of scope for future debate about the balance between government and statute on the one hand and self-regulation on the other. What is certain is that no system of regulation or statute can prevent abuse. All that matters is that abuse is tracked down relatively rapidly and that the guilty suffer consequences.

As the international markets have become more stateless and deregulated there has been more evidence of a willingness to track down large scale fraud and crime and to bring the guilty to book. There have been several scandals concerning insider trading on both sides of the Atlantic. One of the common themes has been the way in which large insider rings hop frontiers to try and reduce the chances of being detected. Whilst many have seen in the growing volume of dismissals of senior people, and of prosecutions, evidence that the financial world is getting more corrupt, others with more

heads have seen that the result of deregulation has been firmer policing. Many of these market practices were going on, perhaps on a
more modest scale, in a more national way, for years. What is now
happening is that moral attitudes have been firmed up, this kind
of twisted dealing has been condemned and the authorities have
at last been prepared to do something to expose it.

The big three markets of the world, London, Tokyo and New
York, are moving closer together. There is more cross-frontier
trading and more common listings of shares and many more common stock issues being offered simultaneously in all three centres.
The message of privatisation has gone home to large multinational
companies, which are also engaged in equity raising across international boundaries. Many other countries are now attempting to
grow their stock markets to catch up or to enjoy some of the benefits
of this explosion of financial entrepreneurship.

The French stock market was already growing prior to the
privatisations, under the impact of the favourable tax inducements
brought in to encourage personal investment. The Loi Monory provided a useful stimulus to private equity investment in France, as
it gave relief from income tax on a fixed amount of saving in equities
each year. Singapore, Australia, New Zealand, Canada and many
other developed countries now embarking on privatisation programmes see one of the advantages as being a broader and deeper
capital market. In turn this will provide more finance for growth
from domestic companies.

Of even more significance is the growing interest of developing
countries in building their stock markets. A successful local stock
market in a heavily indebted country can, as we have seen, assist
greatly in raising domestic savings to rebuild the shattered equity
base of many a local company, or even of the government itself.
A whole series of studies is being undertaken worldwide to see how
these developing countries' stock markets can grow more quickly.
Few of these studies are really necessary. The answer is clear for
all to see in the dramatic growth of the London market under the
impact of deregulation, and especially of major privatisation popular
share issues.

By the end of the 1970s the London market was only raising
£1000 million per annum in new equity for British companies. This
has expanded tenfold in the space of seven years, largely as a result
of the marketing campaigns for the privatisation issues. In the
autumn of 1987 this movement reached the point where a single
issue, British Petroleum, raised nearly eight times the total annual

volume of new equity issues on the Stock Market some eight years earlier, thanks to the underwriters. It has shown conclusively that a stock market can expand dramatically if the conditions are favourable, and if someone is prepared to take the risk and offer large quantities of equity.

The same was proved in Jamaica with the privatisation programme. The Turks, who wished to build a capital market to foster their own economic growth, have spent considerable time and money debating and studying all the rules and preconditions for a successful stock market. Only one thing has so far escaped them, that is, the need for a regular and substantial flow of new issues to the marketplace in order to see it grow and develop of its own accord.

It is possible to spend too much time worrying about rules and administration. There is abundant evidence to suggest that stock markets can get into difficulties over settlement and administration procedures, but the pressure of events that comes from a major equity issuing programme makes it worthwhile finding a solution to those problems. In many stock markets around the world, even in ones where the pressure of dealing is still very light, there are inordinate delays in settlement. It is amazing that it can take six months to issue a share certificate or cash when a transaction dealt with by modern computing power and communications could easily be settled within the space of a week. The London market itself has fallen badly behind in speed of settlements as a result of the great surge of transactions. Huge investment has been made in new technology but it has not kept pace with the volume of business; the effort put into selling shares and developing the commercial side of business has, for the time being, substantially outstripped the amount of thought and effort put into the settlement system itself.

Major advances are often messy and imperfect. There is no sign at the moment that late settlement is acting as a deterrent to dealing in stocks and shares. Nor is it likely to do so. The only thing that would be a major disincentive would be a substantial collapse of companies in a given stock market resulting in substantial losses to investors. This is why forethought about insurance and guarantees concerning settlements can be an important component in the popularisation of the capital market. It is possible to develop systems whereby the market as a whole will stand behind all bargains carried out by licensed practitioners on that exchange. This has to be paid for and has an element of injustice in it, in that the well run businesses can cross-subsidise the less well run. It may, however, be the price that must be paid to ensure that popular capitalism is not tarnished by a major collapse of confidence in any given stock market, through the ultimate failure of the settlement system resulting from the inadequacy of the resources held by the underlying securities houses.

The essence of popular capitalism lies in rejuvenating the cult of the equity and spreading it to countries which have not enjoyed it before. That this is happening is in no small measure due to the combination of privatisation programmes and the liberalisation and technological change driving stock market developments. Sensible countries now see the role stock markets can play in development economics. They wish to have healthy and growing stock markets of their own. There will always be disparaging remarks about the economics of the casino and those who carry equity risk too lightly and sell too quickly at too rapid a profit will always attract disopprobrium. It should never be forgotten, however, that they are also performing a useful economic role in carrying risk and spreading it. There is no written law which says that shares always have to go up or people always have to make profits. The world has been fortunate in that the launch of popular capitalism has taken place against the background of expanding profit margins and expanding markets worldwide. As a result shares have tended to go up and people's first experiences of ownership have been favourable. Some have already been put to the test as in the UK with the precipitate decline of some of the oil shares they purchased, or with the retreat of the British Telecom share price under political attack over its pricing and service quality. Others were put to the test later, when stock markets worldwide decided that enough was enough in the autumn of 1987.

For the moment we can see a developing pattern of growing and flourishing stock markets worldwide coming to play an ever larger role in gathering savings and replacing debt. The Philippines market has awakened from the dead. The Jamaican stock market has expanded beyond recognition from tiny beginnings. The three giant markets of London, New York and Tokyo grow with great speed and purpose. Paris has come alive under the twin pressures of taxation change and privatisation. The message is spreading to other European, Asian and even Latin American markets. It will continue to spread for it is driven by dire necessity.

7

Unburdening the Entrepreneur: Tax Reform in Many Countries

The development of enterprise economies may require tax reform on a grand scale. One of the side effects of massive government intervention in business life over the decades of the 1960s and 1970s throughout the Western world, was the growth of an ever larger taxation system. Governments were not usually content merely to put up the rates of the most basic types of taxes on income and spending. They also used the opportunity to think up a whole variety of new impositions bringing capital gains, capital transfers, gifts, investment income and a variety of other monetary transactions into tax.

Because the overall tax rates on incomes and businesses had to rise so dramatically in order to cope with the enormous increase in government functions and expenditure, there was also consistent lobbying to reduce the total tax burden. Governments sought an easy way out of this dilemma by offering an ever larger array of special reliefs or tax breaks. In part this was a simple response to lobbying pressure. In part it was further evidence of the government's belief that, if government intervened and guided the economy in all its ramifications, its performance would improve. In consequence, in many countries tax incentives were given to businesses to make certain kinds of investment, to individuals to save rather than to spend, or to spend on some things rather than on others. Reliefs were given for mortgages and special kinds of housing. Different categories of people could qualify for different types of relief — if you were married, if you had any children, if you were disabled, if you were saving for your retirement and a whole host of other reasons. The result of granting these reliefs was the need to raise the basic rates of taxation still higher to combat the loss of revenue which resulted as many people used the reliefs and managed their affairs in a way which minimised their tax burden.

By the middle-1980s most Western countries, and many developing countries, had tax systems that were frighteningly complicated. In the UK, for example, in 1979 the marginal rate of tax on investment income was a staggering 98 per cent. The marginal rate of tax on 'earned' income was a stunning 83 per cent. Elsewhere in the world marginal rates of tax in excess of 60 per cent were quite common. In the UK corporation tax on companies was levied at 52 per cent, but most companies with any kind of investment programme, restocking problems or tax losses that could be carried forward, were, in practice, paying an average rate considerably lower than that.

The high tax rates and many tax breaks substantially altered the structure of the economies themselves. At the same time, those few countries or territories which persevered with low tax rates and relatively simple taxation systems attracted a great deal of the mobile money around the world, and not a few of the mobile entrepreneurs. People sought out tax havens like Hong Kong, the Channel Islands, the Bahamas and the few other relatively free economic zones in the world. In the most highly taxed countries the rich either emigrated legally, often taking themselves as well as their tax affairs to another shore, or they evaded the most penal rates of taxation by the returns they made. In developing countries tax was another reason to take capital out of the country, capital which was fleeing the country through fear of political instability or currency weakness or both. It was the age of suitcase money, flowing across frontiers without questions being asked, and the era of bearer bonds purchased by those who wanted to keep their wealth quiet. Swiss and other bankers known for their discretion about these things must have carried on a flourishing business as the money flowed towards them.

The UK first got interested in the general subject of tax reform and simplification in 1983. Following the re-election of the Conservative government the idea of a radical reform of corporate taxes was put on the agenda. It was calculated that if all the reliefs that were allowed for investment, stocks and so forth were scrapped the average corporation tax rate could be brought down from 52 per cent to 35 per cent. Smaller companies, which were always favoured under the old corporation tax regime, could see their corporation tax rate fall to 30 per cent, in line with the standard rate of income tax. This reform was enacted in the 1984 budget. There were predictable howls of protest from those who thought they would lose by the deal. Shipping companies and certain types of industrial company claimed that they would go bankrupt overnight as a result of losing lucrative reliefs. Many complained that the more successful businesses like retail and property, which had been paying rather higher average rates, would benefit at the expense of the shipping and industrial sectors. However, the government put the whole scheme through and the results were startling.

Profits continued a strong recovery. Although there was an investment surge prior to the termination of all the investment reliefs, high levels of investment continued even after the tax breaks had been removed. More importantly, because profits and business confidence were rising, corporation tax receipts continued to shoot upwards although the rate was so much lower. The opposition soon died down and no companies went bankrupt as a result of the change of taxation system.

The most dramatic result was the change of attitudes in many British board rooms. Whereas in the 1970s so much of investment and business life was seen as an adjunct to tax planning, where the critical decisions about investment were based on their taxation consequences for the group as a whole, from the 1980s onwards much more rational decisions were being taken about whether an investment is worthwhile in itself. In some ways the transformation of the corporation tax system was as significant in its impact on British corporate behaviour as the change in union legislation was in freeing so much of British business from the prior and overriding question 'will the unions agree to these changes?'

The US was also contemplating taxation reform. The government decided to change corporate and income taxes together. The US income tax system had even more special allowances built into it than the British one. The Federal administration was able to protect the basic tax reliefs on mortgages and pensions, scrap most of the other reliefs and end up with a much much simpler system with much lower average and marginal rates of tax. The American tax system now has the lowest top tax rate in the world at 27 per cent. Revenues are buoyant and increasing as a result of the strength of the US economy and, no doubt, because the honesty of returns has increased as the rates have fallen. In the UK the decision to reduce the highest rates of tax from 98 per cent and 83 per cent to 60 per cent has also produced a much higher share of revenue from the higher rate taxpayers. This both reflects the fact that some people have decided to come back to England or stay in England who would have migrated abroad before, and that the richer group have been prospering in an era of high returns on investment and encouragement to their entrepreneurship. Both the US and the UK, in their different ways, have demonstrated that simplifying and cutting taxes can assist in the process of economic rejuvenation and can lead to higher rather than lower overall tax receipts.

The impact of taxes upon the structure of an economy can be considerable. In the UK the decision to allow complete tax relief on all monies up to a specified limit paid into a pension fund led to a growing institutional influence of equity and government security investments. By deciding to break out of institutional domination through privatisation the government has been fighting with one hand tied firmly behind its back. For none of the privatisation investments attract tax relief in the hands of the individual buying them whereas all money saved through an institutional pension fund attracts such tax relief.

It was in France that the government first made the decision to encourage individual equity investment through direct tax breaks. We have mentioned elsewhere in this book the importance of the Loi Monory in creating a new class of French shareholder. This process was given a much greater impetus when privatisation too was pitched towards the small investor.

In the UK the first important fiscal change to have a bearing on the balance between institutional and individual investment lay in the pensions field. The government was eventually persuaded that institutional domination of money brought its own dangers in terms of the management of industry and commerce. The government was also persuaded that the origins of this institutional influence lay in the fiscal and administrative rules governing pension funds. In consequence, the decision was made to introduce personal portable pensions. If an individual decides that he does not wish to see all his pension savings husbanded in a large company fund, and run on his behalf without him being able to find out what his own individual assets are worth, he can now opt instead to have his own individual pension fund. This may be run by a professional institutional manager but, at any time, the individual can change the management himself, find out what his assets are worth and expect to have a valuation of his particular shareholdings. This system, when it is fully operational after April 1988, should attract a large number of people, especially those who are naturally rootless or work in new industries where change is the order of the day. This will help reverse the tide in favour of institutional ownership of equities.

The requirements of an enterprise policy can point either in the direction of backing wholesale radical tax reform or towards adding yet more tax allowances to a creaking taxation system. With the exception of the US government, most countries have pursued both routes unevenly at the same time. In the UK a large number of breaks in the tax system have been introduced to allow or encourage enterprise to flourish. The most famous of these was the introduction of the Business Expansion Scheme. Anyone investing out of his earned income could receive a full tax offset for the amount invested if it qualified under the Business Expansion Scheme. Basically, the investment must be in a new or small growing business and the investment cannot be withdrawn for some five years. The investment will not be quoted and the tax relief is only secured permanently once the five years have passed. This scheme attracted moderate amounts of money into a new style of venture capital in the UK, and gave a further stimulus to the growth of a venture capital market. In the 1970s, unlike the US, the UK had practically no venture capital at all. Those thinking of setting up a business either had to resort to family money or the banking system for a loan, or they had no chance of getting started. Now there are a number of venture capital specialists who may either recommend Business Expansion Fund money or have access to larger amounts of institutional money prepared to have a go with a venture capital investment. Any enterprise economy needs a successful venture capital market to fund those businesses that are too small for a main Stock Market quotation but have outgrown family or banking resources.

The UK government removed the tax break that attracted money into life insurance investment schemes. A tax relief at half the standard rate of income tax had been allowed on this type of investment. Its abolition had no more than a temporary impact upon the volume of life insurance transactions but has done something to even up the tax balance between institutional and private investment.

The choice between offering special inducements along the lines of the French Loi Monory or the British Expansion Scheme to encourage equity investment, and having much lower overall rates of tax and allowing people to save as they like, is not an easy one to make when trying to rebuild an enterprise economy. If a country opts for the simplified tax system, people can then make unbiased judgments, unaffected by taxation issues, as to how they wish to save their money or whether they wish to spend or save it in the first place. The world is veering toward tax reform in a big way. The grand example of the US is proving very influential. Many politicians worldwide are now arguing that if the US has such low rates of income taxation they will have to respond. If their tax rates remain high there is a temptation for individuals to move to the US where they can get a high level of net remuneration, or even for whole businesses to decide to move back, or locate there in the first place, so that their executives can be better remunerated. There is a general feeling worldwide that it is better to tax spending rather than income. It is certainly easier to collect taxation on spending as a great deal of spending has to go through the recognised retail sector and it is relatively easy to collect taxes on spending from the retail sector direct. Conversely, income is so fragmented in millions of hands that it is quite difficult to be sure that everyone who is earning income has been taxed. Even if they are in correspondence with the tax authorities they may not have made an honest declaration of all their sources of revenue. There is also a feeling worldwide that it is better to have lower average tax rates and fewer complications. It saves on administration. It produces fewer economic distortions. It is another step in the direction of simplifying and reducing the role of government. The UK decided to go further in cutting higher rates and simplifying taxes in the radical 1988 budget.

Successful tax reform and lower tax rates on income and on investment will be another important element in rebuilding the enterprise economy and fostering faster-growing, better-financed stock markets.

Enterprise and economic recovery

One of the common characteristics of countries experiencing an economic revival through liberalisation, privatisation and the other techniques dealt with above is that the economic recovery is often patchy in its impact and extent. Many countries have experienced unreasonably high levels of unemployment throughout the 1980s. The 1981 recession was particularly severe and many countries at that time experienced a labour shake-out from traditional industries, or from the public services, or both, which has proved difficult to mop up as the economy recovers. The Japanese economy has been least affected by this process. It has a very strong infrastructure of highly competitive small businesses that continue to supply the bulk of job opportunities in Japan. The very few large trading houses and big industrial conglomerates at the top have largely adhered to their policy of adapting their workforce to new skills within the enterprise itself and have not, on the whole, laid off large numbers of people. Above all the Japanese experience has been based on the formidable strength of Japan as a trading nation, capable of out-exporting and out-competing most of the countries of the world. In consequence, it has been the most successful economy at generating jobs and retaining them. It has been assisted in this process by the strong links between a dedicated government industrial culture and the myriad of small competing firms. Small businesses deliver the parts at low cost and on time. The great trading houses assemble and sell them.

The US economy was the second most successful of the large countries. It developed a major unemployment problem in 1981/82 during the recession but it bounced back sharply and proved itself capable of spawning a very large number of service sector activities requiring a large amount of new labour. The results were soon seen in a rapid decline in unemployment towards more acceptable levels.

In contrast, all of the major Western European economies experienced great difficulty. At the time of writing, the only large European economy to have experienced any success in reversing the trend of unemployment is the UK where jobs have been expanding for some four years and unemployment has been falling for eighteen months. France, Germany, Italy, Spain and the other leading countries have had a more uneven experience. Their economies have proved much more resistant to the creation of new business and, in consequence, without the infrastructure of small expanding service sector companies as in Japan and the US, they have found that unemployment remains obstinately high. In Australia and New Zealand, also following the new economic policies, unemployment has remained a great difficulty. In New Zealand the successful, enterprising economies of the cities have leapt ahead and have created new employment opportunities, but these have been insufficient to offset the great job losses from the traditional industries and from the relatively poor rural areas.

The UK has suffered from a particularly malign case of differential rates of recovery and improvement on a regional and geographical basis. For several years now there has been talk of a North/South divide. The rapid growth and apparent prosperity of the South East has been contrasted with the difficulties of the North. However, closer observation of the figures, and of the physical landscape, has revealed that the divide is not a simple

North/South one. The contrast lies between the urban areas, usually at or close to the centres of the large industrial cities, and the rest of the country. More than half a dozen boroughs close to the City of London have unemployment rates around 20 per cent, very low average incomes per head and considerable physical dereliction on the ground. Areas close to the centre of Manchester have similar intense problems, whilst much of Liverpool is a wasteland punctuated by tower block council estates. There have been similar problems in large chunks of Teeside and Tyneside and in some of the Yorkshire and Lancashire textile towns.

Much of the rest of the North is every bit as prosperous as the typical southern market town. A town like Harrogate in Yorkshire, which has traditionally relied upon tourism and leisure, has responded well to the new circumstances, building a thriving conference trade. It has done a much better job in adjusting to the new lifestyle and market opportunities than many southern resort towns which have lost their traditional holiday business. Compared with Hastings or Ramsgate, Harrogate is a thriving town with low unemployment, many new facilities and a big leisure trade, and the southern towns are less affluent with unemployment well over 15 per cent and a relatively low average income per head.

The problem has been that enterprise capitalism has passed by on the other side when it comes to remaining in, or rejuvenating, the inner city areas that are most obviously derelict. Some would say this demonstrates that giving enterprise its head merely serves to heighten inequalities and fails to deal with the deep underlying social problems which only government action can tackle. However, further analysis of the problem shows that much of the difficulty in those urban areas lies in the very government action that has been undertaken, often by municipal authorities. Each of those rundown urban areas has the same characteristics: a very high proportion of the land and housing is in public ownership, a large amount of public money has been spent on extensive urban renewal projects, particularly in the late 1960s, creating a bleak and daunting landscape. Now millions of pounds of public money is poured in to prop up the hard-pressed welfare services dealing with a population which has above average levels of sickness, unemployment and old age.

The worst problems lie where industry has let the community down by allowing the collapse of the principal factory at the same time that the over-municipalisation of life has fostered bad rehousing and poor rehabilitation schemes. The combination of the decline of a principal industry and bad municipal policies creating the wrong kind of environment succeeds in driving out many of the enterprising and talented people from the local community. The result is that the enterprising people move to market towns or to the rural south where they set up their new businesses and buy their new homes. Local planners prevent private housing being constructed which could change the social mix of the community and return some community leaders to the urban area. Planners also turn down the requests of those who wish to build offices or high-tech buildings near the centres of our large cities. Politics dictates that only traditional manufacturing industries can be sited in some areas. In consequence some local authorities shut the door on all the new styles of enterprise and business that could bring jobs and much needed cash back into circulation in the local urban economy.

It has been an obstinate irony of British life that some of the poorest parts of the country lie only a 50p bus ride away from one of the richest areas of real estate in the world, the twin cities of Westminster and London. Yet it is true that the areas of Lambeth, Southwark, Tower Hamlets, Hackney, Stepney, Bow and the other inner London boroughs so close to the City of London are amongst the poorest areas of Western Europe and economic activity does not spread from the one to the other because markets have been deliberately stamped out. The welfare culture is all-pervasive and people are trapped in a cycle of deprivation and welfarism. The Conservative government is now attempting to demonstrate that even in these hard-bitten cases, popular capitalism can have its impact. The paradox is that because state action is responsible for so much of the activity and ownership in the area it takes state action to get the thing right. The government has been prepared to live with the paradox in the interests of getting things done. The establishment of the London Docklands Development Corporation has been the pioneering example, now of great interest worldwide, showing how government can start to undo the sins of commission and omission perpetrated by other government bodies.

In order to break the stranglehold of the boroughs over 5500 acres of undesirable real estate close to the City of London, the government gave this new government body, the London Docklands Development Corporation, power to acquire and to develop land within those geographical confines. These powers override those of the local authority and often entail the Docklands Development Corporation acquiring the land compulsorily from the local authority or from the Port of London Authority which had presided over the collapse of the docks. Once the Development Corporation has acquired the land it can then spend money on cleaning it up and putting in any necessary infrastructure like roads and telecommunications. It attracts private developers who are prepared to build offices, flats, houses, light commercial property and retail space. The gearing impact has been phenomenal. For every £1 of public money spent some £10 of private capital is now being attracted. Land values have started to soar and a development bonanza is underway. The government should be able to get all its money back over a ten year period as it turns from being a net buyer of land to being a net seller of it. The government need, at the end, own nothing at all in Docklands as it will be a totally rebuilt self-sufficient community with a wide diversity of housing, industry, high-tech and commercial activity and good shopping areas.

So successful has the Docklands experiment been in breaking through the red tape and the socialised quagmire, that this system is now being applied to other parts of the country. Development corporations are being set up in parts of Manchester, Birmingham, Teeside, Tyneside and there was already one on Merseyside. These are the chosen agents to bring enterprise and private capital back into these areas and to create once again balanced communities with a mixture of public and private housing where before only the municipal landlord reigned.

It is important to popular capitalism that it can demonstrate that it has something to contribute in the toughest conditions. Its proponents have to be able to counter-argue the proposition that all free enterprise is good for the rich and bad for the poor and serves only to divide a country. In New Zealand the liberalising Labour Party is going to have to think of a similar answer to the problems of relative rural deprivation now that it is doing such a good job in releasing the energies of the cities, making them into magnets for capital and people. It is fascinating to observe the difference between New Zealand and the UK, with people in the UK fleeing the cities for the suburban and rural areas to find prosperity while in New Zealand the reverse is happening. In both cases planning and enterprise policies themselves have to be adjusted to create a better balance and avoid the charge of division.

At the outset attitudes towards the Docklands experiment were as sceptical as those of the critics of privatisation towards the idea of introducing private capital into nationalised industries. In the mid-1970s, when research on what could be done to rejuvenate the dying Docklands areas of East London first began, the response came very clearly and firmly from the surveyors, architects and property specialists in the City that East London would never work and would always be unattractive to the private sector. At that stage the City of London ended abruptly a few blocks to the east of the Bank of England. Property specialists in the mid-1970s were even prepared to venture that Cannon Street was not prime property, although it contained a principal station serving the City and was a very short walk from Mansion House Square, the heart of the financial district.

It was the insurance brokers who first began to demonstrate that the City could spread eastwards and that the prosperity need not remain confined forever within a single square mile. The very high cost of premises and their need to take on more staff to transact a growing volume of business took them further eastwards, even beyond the Tower of London itself. They spread out to the Minories and Aldgate. A leading development company, Taylor Woodrow, took on the task of refurbishing St Catherines Dock by the Tower and created, out of an old dock and run down warehouses, a delightful international trade centre, a small boat marina and a large hotel which, after a few years, was trading very profitably. They too had met with scepticism, with many predicting that the hotel was too far east ever to make money.

Once the London Docklands Corporation got under way, under the charismatic dual leadership of Nigel Broakes, the Chairman of Trafalgar House, and Bob Mellish, a former Labour MP for a Docklands constituency, things started to move much more quickly to penetrate further and further eastwards. The insurance brokers had shown the way. Private housing developers began to understand that, with the very low price of land available in the early days in Docklands, they could erect good brick houses, sell them at £30,000 or £40,000 each and make a profit, when comparable London houses would sell at twice that or more. The sceptics maintained that no one would buy them because they were too far east. Yet, when the first houses became available at these prices, people queued all night or even for a week, in order to be first in the queue to make sure they could secure one.

It was often argued that no one who had lived in the old docklands would ever benefit from this process of rejuvenation. The houses and jobs, it was claimed, would go to others. Yet there were many examples of people in council houses in the docklands boroughs, or on the waiting lists of the docklands boroughs, who took advantage of the priority system to buy their own home. It was true that many of the jobs and houses went to people from outside the docklands area, but opportunities expanded enormously. The absence of some docklands people from the lists of those taking the jobs reflects more on the welfare benefits system in the UK than it does on the principle of making the employment available for those with all kinds of skills and those with none.

Over the years the Docklands Corporation demonstrated considerable vision. It understood earlier than most professionals that Docklands was a great opportunity which could become a thriving and prosperous city in its own right. The decision to site major leisure facilities and to build an airport in Docklands provided a necessary focus for this redevelopment and captured the imagination of those contemplating a Docklands investment. The waterside was very attractive once people began to see that it need not be mud and oil slicks for ever. Filling in the riverside from the Tower of London to the beautiful buildings in Greenwich was the most exciting architectural and planning challenge in London since the Great Fire and Christopher Wren's seventeenth century reconstruction.

It was one of the ironies of modern enterprise capitalism that it took government intervention and vision to get the thing started, for it had taken so much government intervention and union wrongheadedness to kill the docks through the Port of London Authority and to kill the inner London boroughs through endless municipalised housing developments and refusal to grant development permits. The experiment now shows that popular capitalism can rebuild in the most difficult and hostile of territories. Far from being divisive or doing people down, popular capitalism has got something to offer to all of the people. Many pilgrims are now wending their way to Docklands and are mastering the street names of the new city. Perhaps one day Heron Quay, Mudchute and Canary Wharf will be names as well known worldwide as Trafalgar Square, Marble Arch and Charing Cross. Certainly London has shown that the bracing enterprise that has rebuilt several rundown American city areas can thrive even in the most socialised of urban areas.

8

Conclusion

It is strange to see views once considered heterodox and even zany gradually coming into fashion. The ideas I set out on the involvement of government and industry, the need to rejuvenate enterprise and break monopolies in the public sector, were ideas culled from the British experience of the early 1970s. They were ideas for one country.

Their origins lay first and foremost in the dreadful experiences during the last eighteen months of Edward Heath's Conservative government from 1972 to early 1974. That government was constantly being held to ransom by powerful trade union monopolies. Many trade unions in central public utilities enjoyed monopoly powers because they had been granted them by the Acts of Parliament nationalising their industries. The Heath government fell because of the nationalised industry trade union problem. Its handling of the problem was incompetent, not to say insensitive. Its political judgement was faulty in believing it could fight a single-subject election against a background of growing public sympathy for the miners and central confusion over the government and National Coal Board case. None the less, many shared a sense that it was unjust that a democratically elected government could be brought down by a powerful group of monopolist trade unionists. The shadow of the miners' victory lay over British politics for a decade from that fateful February in 1974 when the Heath government met its understandable fate at the hands of the British electorate.

It would be wrong to say that those of us who worried about this problem simply wished to avenge the defeat. None of us, I hope, had in mind such an unpleasant and violent sequel as finally took place under the regime of Mr Scargill: his leadership of the mine workers' union created the protracted and difficult pit dispute of the summer of 1984. But it was that major event in British politics of the early 1970s that led me to write and think and try and proselytise in favour of breaking up monopoly concentrations of power, wherever they lay, but especially in the public sector, and introducing private capital on some scale or other into these large public enterprises.

There were several harbingers, forerunners and fathers of the idea. The Institute of Economic Affairs had always kept alight a small but important flame for free enterprise economics throughout the post-war period. So too Aims of Industry, often maligned as extreme in its views, bravely battled on and had gained considerable support from some influential industrialists in favour of restoring some sanity to a distorted marketplace. Rhodes Boyson had written in favour of these ideas during the Heath government. Yet the core political traditions of the country were against such ideas as late as 1979. The Conservative manifesto of that year made no mention of wholesale privatisation nor the role of private capital in rejuvenating the economy. Neither that manifesto, nor the 1983 manifesto, made any observations about the way in which overseas and government-to-government lending for overseas projects was failing, and how new initiatives might be needed in development economics.

From 1979 onwards there was always the chance that the Conservative government in the UK would make some brave decisions in favour of restoring some elements of the marketplace to areas dominated by public monopoly. In the opposition years the Shadow transport spokesman had drafted a bus deregulation bill, although it took five years in government before that work was to come to fruition. In opposition it had been agreed that the nationalised oil, aerospace and ship building industries would be returned to the private sector, although portions of the ship building industry still remain public to this day. It was a long and protracted battle before even the warship building yards could be sold back to private owners. The signal advance was the decision by Sir Keith Joseph to privatise British Telecom. That one decision transformed privatisation from a minor matter of selling a few bits and pieces of state ironmongery to a few willing buyers into a major programme with enormous social and economic ramifications.

In 1983, following the victory at the polls, it was possible to build a much bigger programme. The decision on British Telecom allowed the government to put together many other suggestions around this bold departure, and to turn piecemeal scrappy privatisation into a broad wide ranging programme. As elsewhere in the world the difficulties in reconciling revenue with expenditure in the government accounts provided considerable impetus to those of us arguing for a large programme, and helped by enabling it to be built into the framework of the national budget. It became something all wings of the Conservative Party could agree on, left and right, as it made available more money both for spending programmes and for the tax cuts dear to the hearts of both sections of the party.

The British Telecom issue did more than just enable Britain to establish the world's first large scale privatisation programme. It also led by chance to the invention of part of popular capitalism. As shown above (Chapter 6), the only way to be sure of a great success in the marketplace was to attract a new wave and generation of investors. The idea of seeking a large new generation of small savers came out of the exigencies of a marketing campaign to sell the world's largest ever equity offering, an equity offering some ten times the size of the traditional large offering on the London market.

Even this idea was greeted with a certain amount of scepticism. Rapidly new obstacles were brought forward. It would not be possible to keep such a large share register. There was a technical limit on the number of share certificates and allocation letters that could be sent out. But, none the less, the government wisely insisted on mass marketing the British Telecom shares and the issue was a triumphant success.

It was only after this the full significance of what had been done became clear. Conservatives in the UK, like Democrats and Republicans in the US, had for years seen the importance of freedom to the societies in which we live. Many philosophers and some politicians had paid lip-service, in their books and speeches, to the idea of political and economic liberty being inextricably entangled. Yet in the sale of British Telecom there was more than the idea: here was the reality of democratic capitalism on the march. At last the prospect opened up, not merely of individuals owning a direct stake in the country through the ownership of their own land and houses, but also through direct ownership of a part of industry itself.

The 1984 miners' strike was another important political watershed for the UK. It was a bloody and unpleasant battle; the violence of the miners shocked many and guaranteed that they enjoyed none of the strong public sympathy for their cause that they had enjoyed under Joe Gormley a decade earlier. It was seen by many at the time, not least by the Prime Minister, as a triumph for democracy itself against the forces of misrule, mob-rule and violence. The law was not to be intimidated. The government of the realm should not be dragged into an industrial dispute unnecessarily. Above all, more money was not going to be found simply to bail out an industry which had long since lost contact with reality, its customers and its marketplace.

These were still events in one country. But from 1985 onwards the steady trickle of overseas visitors to London became a torrent. The world was aware, in the early days, that something significant was happening in London which had wide implications for the world economy as a whole. They were often ahead of British commentators in appreciating the significance of it all. Those early visitors in 1984 and 1985 were cautious and sceptical. Whilst they recognised the British achievement they, like the progenitors of that achievement, saw it then as an experience relevant to Britain alone. Many argued that it was only possible in a country with an advanced capital market like that in London. Many thought the liberalisation and privatisation programme only relevant in a country as heavily socialised and with the unique labour history of Britain. Many saw it as right wing politics of a kind that their own middle-of-the-road socialist societies could not accept. But others were more impressed and gradually the message started filtering around the world.

The French opposition were most interested. The new ideas fitted directly with their kind of politics. They needed an antidote to the new wave of Mitterand nationalisations following the presidential socialist victory in 1981. They listened, they learned and they adapted the experience to French conditions. The Canadians were intrigued and got to work on studying their own situation in more detail. They were interested, not merely in privatisation itself, but in the mechanisms of government by which it had been delivered, carrying the possibility of reform into the very core of the Canadian cabinet office and prime ministerial entourage. The Turks were fascinated and started conducting their own domesday book survey of the Turkish parastatal economy. The Italians and the Spaniards were pursuing their own independent solutions to the problems of large and rambling industrial holding companies built up by their respective governments over the preceeding 40 years. They soon turned to the path of selective divestment with accelerating programmes in 1986.

It was the victory of Jacques Chirac in France, early in 1986, which gave the world its second large and important privatisation programme. The French programme proceeded more swiftly than the British, learning from British mistakes.

But, to be relevant to the debt problem of the developing world, the techniques of popular capitalism and privatisation needed to be transferred to more hostile climates. The sale of the National Commercial Bank of Jamaica in November of 1986 was the first pioneering offer for sale on popular capitalism lines in any Third World country. Overnight it increased the number of shareholders on the island sixfold and brought in two and a half times the amount of annual turnover of the stock exchange in 1985. It demonstrated that popular capitalism was a mechanism by which savings could be accumulated and invested in industrial and commercial activity in a developing country.

The second important breakthrough took place in project finance. Project finance has a long-standing history. The American banks, after all, had taught the British many of its skills in the early 1970s, when they applied American techniques for project finance lending to the rapid development of the North Sea oil fields. Natural resource projects worldwide, whether gold mines or oil wells, copper mines or rubber plantations, had traditionally been financed in the private sector on a project financing basis. In the mid-1980s new developments occurred bringing project finance to the centre of the arguments over the vexed question of the relations between government and private finance.

Again, some of the pioneering work was done in Britain. The circumstances were, as usual, typically British. The government was wedded to the notion that it could not increase public expenditure rapidly as it wished to reduce taxes to restore the spirit of enterprise in the economy. Nor did it wish to expand the budget deficit unduly, although it was under enormous pressure to do so in the early years of its life. Yet it was also under continuing pressure from those who argued that the infrastructure of the country was not receiving enough investment capital, that the sewers were crumbling, the roads degenerating and that something should be done about it.

Looking at the problem during the early 1980s it seemed intractable. Try as the government might to reduce revenue expenditure it never succeeded. The resulting pressures on the budget meant that it was difficult to expand capital investment as rapidly as the government might have liked, whilst much of the capital investment in the public sector was of a dubious utility in the industrial world — evidence showed that in the past such investment had often been misguided and never earned a positive return. Privatisation of industries was part of the answer as it transferred the investment burden in the main utility services away from the government sector into private hands operating in the bracing environment of the marketplace. But the question of the adequacy and the method of financing infrastructure investment remained.

I am amazed at how long it took to see one possible way through. For years some had said that things could be built in the private sector and financed privately. Yet such projects had always fallen down on two grounds. First, the private sector projectors were usually keen to avoid any real risk of their own, always writing in copious government guarantees to any scheme they put forward. Secondly, the Treasury was adamant that infrastructure like roads and sewers had to be financed publicly and there was no way round the Treasury rules.

An important battle occurred over the bridge or tunnel at Dartford. The completion of the six-lane M25 link around London was bound to expose the total inadequacy of a four-lane highway across the Thames on the eastern section of the M25 outer-orbital road. There was not enough money in the roads budget for a government financed tunnel or bridge to be constructed. It was agreed that one had to be built and a competition was arranged. After much agonising and discussion it was somewhat reluctantly conceded that the option of private finance could also be included in the tenders submitted. The Treasury remained deeply sceptical on two counts: it was thought that the private contractors would not take adequate risk and that the private financing would end up costing more than public sector finance for the scheme.

These two arguments were inconsistent. Of course if a projector bears specific risks on a project the cost of his finance is going to be higher than if the government borrows the money secured against tax-payers' revenue. In a way the extra interest rate is a direct assessment of the risk the private sector projector is bearing compared with the risk-free cost of finance whose proxy is best measured by the government borrowing rate. Yet here was the Treasury arguing both that the private sector should carry some specific risk, and that it should not pay for it, otherwise the project would be dearer than in the public sector.

There was a further piece of sophistry in the argument. Of course, the apparent cost of the project to the government would be the cost of risk-free capital. Yet across the public sector, over many years, a whole variety of projects financed with so called risk-free money had been invested in projects which were extremely risky, where most of the capital had been lost in addition to the costs of the interest charges. In order to calculate the true cost of government capital on similar projects it would be necessary to work out the actual investment experience and to include in the cost the large write-downs and write-offs that have characterised so much government investment in industrial and infrastructure projects.

The Dartford debate was an interesting one. The resulting victory for those favouring private project finance was the most singular reversal of Treasury orthodoxy of the last decade. It has eased the way in the UK for a whole range of imaginatively financed infrastructure projects channelling savers' money directly, or through the hands of intermediary banks, into what would previously have been tax-payer financed projects. The Treasury, however, is still trying to assert its Ryrie doctrine which makes such prospects difficult.

This innovation has a bearing elsewhere in the world as well. It is leading governments worldwide to ask themselves the question: does this function have to remain in the public sector? And if we don't wish to privatise can we none the less introduce private capital and private competition, perhaps through project financing some new investment?

The third important innovation helping to ease the plight of the heavily indebted nations was the painful and gradual evolution of a market in Third World debt. It was clear from the outset of the debt crisis that a market solution was needed. It was necessary to find out what the debt might be worth, how people and investors generally measured the risk of particular countries and principalities. There had to be a mechanism whereby banks which felt over-encumbered with certain kinds of difficult debt could free themselves of it and regain some of the capital they had ventured. The evolution of debt swap has already made a sizeable impact on the mountain of Chilean debt and is spreading rapidly in Mexico, in the Philippines, the Caribbean and elsewhere. The newest development is to link a debt swap directly to a privatisation. Thus a foreign investor can be attracted, he can purchase overseas debt of the country concerned, the central bank can arrange for its cancellation and, in return, the foreign investor can be given assets from the state industrial sector. At one and the same time losses can be reduced on the revenue account as a loss-making business is passed to a new investor, and the interest burden on the external account can be cut as the external investor buys in and the central bank cancels the overseas debt.

Everywhere around the world the same message is sinking in. It is free enterprise which generates wealth and prosperity. It is through competitive markets that a range of providers jostle for position and compete to innovate, invest and flourish. The power of policies of deregulation and introducing competition is being seen worldwide. The buses in England and Jamaica have been deregulated. Airlines around the world are beginning to feel the pressure of competitive forces with new independent airlines on domestic UK routes, with US routes revolutionised by strong competition, and even the European airlines now subject to the forces of change under the stimulus of the EEC's competition directive.

This policy is linked directly to the stimulation of small business and small enterprise. Much of the growth of employment in the US, and in those territories in Europe where it is growing, has come from the small enterprise sector. The world is rediscovering the incentive which owning and running a business can provide. It is rediscovering the flexibility of small business units and the unique relationship between the small business and its customer. Development economics is now centring on building a strong small-company culture in countries where, in the past, the answers have been sought through state enterprise on a massive scale.

Small enterprise, competition, new sources of business activity are all part of the story. Money to invest through the phenomenal expansion of the eurobond market, routing investors' savings direct into businesses on a worldwide scale, helped bridge the gap in the late 1970s and early 1980s. The later 1980s and the early 1990s will be a period of renewed enthusiasm for direct equity investment. It is to stock markets that the world is again turning, to channel investor savings direct into productive enterprise. Without the intermediation of the stockmarket there is no extra credit creation caused by the banks on lending deposit holders' money. Equity or direct investment means an investor buys with money he saved or earned and takes his own risk. If the equity investment goes wrong, he loses. It does not of itself bring down the banking system or threaten worldwide financial Armageddon. If the return on capital is high enough on average, the investors will do well. One of the characteristics of the last three years has been the steady improvement in the rate of return on capital worldwide after a period in the 1970s when inflation in the leading Western industrial nations reduced the real rate of return and often made it negative.

The surge of interest in building stock markets is now apparent in many a developing country. In China, the home of second generation communism, people are turning again to capitalist solutions. The Shanghai stock exchange opened for the first time since the revolution towards the end of 1986 and, early in 1987, the Beijing stock exchange also reopened. Simultaneously China announced a programme of turning many of its state enterprises into public limited companies, floating some of their shares for private investors to purchase.

The creation of great global financial markets trading around the clock from Japan to New York via London has brought with it problems of international policing and regulation. The scale and pace of the change has taken many aback. Where some five years ago it was only the visionary who talked about a huge, around the world, around the clock stock market, now such talk is commonplace. The technology of telephones, screens and data banks is in place. Traders are coming to grips with a world where they are only awake and active for one-third of the time during which the stocks they are interested in are traded. On the American business television programme at breakfast there is an up to date report on how the American dollar and American stocks are trading in London before Wall Street has opened. On Japanese television there are market reports from London and New York about the state of the Yen and the leading Japanese companies. London remains a central entrepôt, poised delicately between the time zones, and with the inestimable advantage of being good at the universal business language of the new stock exchanges, English.

The pattern of regulation has so far been desultory. The US tried the statutory system but it has produced little joy and great expense. The UK is experimenting with a self-regulatory system, but that too is encountering considerable difficulty in counteracting the scale and range of fraud in the newly sensitive world that worries about insider trading, illegal deals and fraudulent purchases of securities. It is no bad thing that there is a quickened interest in the legality of deals and that some of the worst practices of the moribund but money-making exchanges of the 1960s and 1970s should be re-examined and made illegal. But there is a need to ensure that the enthusiasm for regulation and statutory control does not end up killing the very process by which wealth creation can be restored and capital generated for the development of the Third World and the Western countries themselves. Capitalism is, by its very nature, an imperfect process because it is an entirely human process. Many of the great advances in the world have combined luck and fast dealing.

In his early days, a future great entrepreneur who will one day join the establishment of the country in which he plies his trade, is often indistinguishable from the fringe elements of the business fraternity. There has to be some modest degree of tolerance and understanding, whilst, at the same time, the international agencies need to agree an international framework of practice and conduct. Big-time crooks should now be pursued across frontiers and through numbered bank accounts. The worst offenders must be caught and brought to book. It is an encouraging sign that in the London market, after years of inactivity, some spectacular insider dealers have now been revealed and action taken against them. As markets broaden, deepen and become more popular so too the authorities have to see that there are standards and a morality enforced through the law of the land and through the international agencies.

The conclusion to this book is that the mechanisms are already in place which can do a great deal to lift Western Europe out of its economic stagnation and stimulate growth and adventure in the developing countries. Their poverty has been made to appear all the more oppressive by the magnitude of their debt crisis and by the early comparisons between the richest and the poorest nations of the world. It is to free enterprise and free enterprise democracy that the world must turn. State socialism and the successful export of Soviet-style communism has failed. Around the world people are rightly sceptical of state-led solutions, state enterprises and endless regulation and control. Markets can again be given their head. On the back of a genuinely popular capitalism it might be possible to build many more freedom-loving, respectable democracies. I remain extremely sceptical of those wise heads in the West who say that democracy is a luxury the Third World cannot afford, or a doctrine we should be cautious about exporting. Whilst democracy is imperfect it is still the best system of government on offer and we should be proud of it. We must understand that the underpinnings of any free democracy are those of a free economy.

There are hazards in plenty. The crash of all the world's stockmarkets in October 1987 showed what can happen to confidence and to people's savings when global technology amplifies pessimism about economic prospects. A sharp, expensive, salutary lesson in risk has been meted out to old and new investors alike, and has administered the first check to the long march of popular capitalism. As more Third World countries encourage new equity investment, the old hazard of compulsory nationalisation without compensation will again rear its head. These and other hazards need not be terminal.

What then, is popular capitalism? Popular capitalism is a series of economic and political ideas that are sweeping the world. The essence of popular capitalism is the belief in the powers and responsibilities of the individual and in the advantages of the marketplace to organise producers and consumers. The strands of popular capitalism are varied. Many of them emanate from the revolution in economic policy undertaken by Margaret Thatcher's government in the UK. Others emanate from the ineluctable logic of the banks, large international companies and governments as they seek to escape from the terrible debt crisis that threatens to engulf them all.

All of the initiatives point in the direction of more sources of equity rather than debt to finance enterprise. They lead to more individuals and families becoming empowered by ownership and management control over resources. The most breathtaking example of how far this thinking has gone in travelling the world is to look at the economic experiments under way in the communist countries of China and Russia themselves. Both, in their distinctive ways, are desperately trying to create a pricing and market system. Both need to do so because state planning, regulation and bureaucracy has let the people down. Living standards have fallen far behind successful enterprise economies in the West. The state system has not even been able to guarantee feeding all of the people all of the time, or producing the type of weapons the state believes it needs to be sure of its defence.

The link with liberty is at its most obvious in the projected Russian reforms. It is no coincidence that, at the same time that Communist Party leader Mikhail Gorbachev is introducing some of the freedoms of the marketplace, he is attempting to encourage some limited criticism, discussion, debate and even choice in elections. For he realises that part of the vitality of the free enterprise system comes from allowing people to generate ideas, and from giving them their heads so that they can prosper. In the West the link is being forged through the process of popular capitalist sales of assets from the state to private individuals. It is more than an economic movement. It is the deliberate intention of the policy to grant to individuals the rights and powers that shareholders enjoy, so that many more people can have a direct stake in, and say over, the affairs of large industrial and commercial companies within their own countries. It has to be reinforced by breaking monopolies, cutting taxes, stimulating enterprise.

Many political philosophers and politicians have perceived the essential bond between property and freedom. For years in the UK, one of the first countries to travel the democratic road, most people believed that you should only have a vote if you had a stake in the kingdom through property ownership. The opening up of a mass franchise to all those who toiled by hand or brain, but did not own their own house and had no share in their business, was a radical departure of the late nineteenth and early twentieth centuries. What the new Conservatives are saying is that it was right to enfranchise every man, but that he will only be truly enfranchised as a full citizen in the economic life of the country when he also has a stake in its land and its means of production.

Experiments by socialists to empower the people by nationalising the main assets of the country failed almost universally. Nationalisation not only failed to deliver the goods in an economic sense, unable to reassure employees, delivering a strike-torn present, never a strike-free future; but it also failed to give the large body of electors any meaningful say or choice over the way the business was run or the kinds of products and service it could deliver.

Popular capitalism puts this right. If you want to see it as a series of images there have been many moving ones in the last few years. You can see it in the faces and the shouts of joy on the streets of Manila when Cory Aquino claimed victory in the elections and announced that she was going to liberate the Philippine people. Her liberation is planned to stretch far beyond the confines of free democratic debate into the very heartlands of the economy through a redistribution of land and a major share selling programme.

You can see it in the eyes and in the conversations of the new army of small shareholders turning up at the British Gas or the British Telecom AGMs in the UK. They will tell you that their opinions have changed; they have been tempered by the process of ownership. At last they feel part of the organisation.

You can see it in the attitudes and the enthusiasms of the lorry drivers of the British National Freight Corporation, who bought out their own lorry business. Because they are confident of their new power as owner/drivers, they voted not to have worker representatives on the Board and to invest overseas as well as in the UK. They did so because they know that, should anything go wrong they, and they alone, are in the position to change the management of the enterprise itself.

You can hear it in the speeches and the programme of deregulation and economic liberation being pursued by the Labour government in New Zealand. As they heroically fight to open areas of public monopoly up to competitive pressures they have, in the forefront of their minds, the vision of accelerating the growth of prosperity in their country and putting more goods and services under a market test so that the customers are better looked after.

For popular capitalism is a large movement whose time has come. It is not yet possible to see how.far or how fast it will spread. The present evidence is that in every country in the world politicians and civil servants will have to react one way or another to these powerful ideas. So far, those who have welcomed them most widely have had the greatest degree of success. All are beginning to see that the world is in a mood for more political freedom through the ballot box and through a free press. It is also seeking more economic liberty through privatisation, deregulation and getting out of debt into equity.

Popular capitalism is nothing short of a major world revolution. The politicians who try to resist it will be tossed aside like trees in a hurricane.

Postscript

Almost eighteen months have elapsed since I wrote the text of the hard-back edition of *Popular Capitalism*. Since September 1987 many of the trends identified in the book have continued apace. The direction of events has been unsurprising: it has been the speed with which they have unfolded that has been startling.

The late 1980s are years of simultaneous democratic revolutions. Europe showed the way in the 1970s. Democracy came to Greece and Portugal in 1974 and to Spain in 1975. Europe from Portugal to Finland and through Greece to Turkey is now democratic or developing an approach to elections and civil liberties that characterises true democracy. Canada, the USA and Mexico make the North American continent a bulwark of freedom. In the 1980s South America, Brazil, Bolivia, Uruguay and Argentina are taking steps towards democracy whilst Peru, Colombia, Ecuador and some of the other smaller countries are already democratic states.

Towards the close of 1988, Chile held a plebiscite on whether the dictatorship of General Pinochet should continue. Despite the very considerable propaganda machinery of the state, and despite the effective campaigning of the General's supporters against communist insurgency, the people voted No, taking Chile a hesitant step down the road towards full democracy. Chile has always been an enigma. It is a country follow-ing the freer economic policies of the democratic world with great success and enthusiasm, yet it has coupled these with a repressive attitude towards civil liberties. This is born of its history, where a severe com-munist regime had thrown up a military alternative. The people of Chile are now trying to tread the path back to full democracy, which lies deep in their history and traditions. Progress may be hesitant, as the General is reluctant to relinquish power despite the vote. The opposition politicians have to demonstrate that they can unite behind a single leader and a truly democratic programme.

On the other side of the world, the Pacific Basin has been in ferment. The well-established democracies of New Zealand, Australia and India now have new allies in the Philippines, South Korea, the Burmese revo-lution and now in the successful conduct of elections in Pakistan. The pattern has been similar in many Pacific countries. Peoples have grown tired of autocratic regimes and have taken to the streets, trying to mimic the people's power of Cory Aquino's successful peaceful revolution. Sometimes it takes the form of labour disputes, sometimes of street protests demanding a new constitution or a change of government. The intention is always the same — democratic reform of the state.

The successful conduct of the elections in Pakistan is heartening for western observers. The brutal end to the Bhutto regime was mirrored in the assassination of President Zia who had taken over as an autocrat. The result of the free elections in November 1988 produced no overall control, but Mr Bhutto's daughter emerged as the most charismatic popular leader at the head of the largest party. The Pakistani democratic constitution is creaking back into life.

This leaves the world with 60 more or less democratic regimes compared to around 100 dictatorships. Even at the heart of the dictatorships in the Soviet Union and China, major changes are under way. When the great movements within communism are taken into account, Africa is left as the unreformed centre of autocracy within an otherwise rapidly liberalising world.

In the summer of 1988 I visited the Far East and included in my itinerary a stop in Shanghai. China is going through a period of ideological meltdown. Many of the old refrains have been cast aside. A struggle is under way between the reformers wishing to place more emphasis upon markets and prices, and the traditionalists wishing to protect the old heavily subsidised, heavily regulated system. Reform has already gone some way in generating a new spirit of small enterprise. Spreading from the farms which were reformed in the late 1960s and early 1970s, small capitalist businesses are now being set up in a variety of service and manufacturing areas. The state is actively considering major changes to its nationalised industries, including incentives, profit motivation and even the disposal of shares.

China has to respond to the opportunity and the threat presented by 1997 in Hong Kong. The wealth and power of Hong Kong is out of all proportion to the relative size of its population. Average incomes per head in Hong Kong are some thirty times higher than those on the mainland of China. Canton is trying to catch up by a major programme of reform, and the coastal strip stretching along the shore adjacent to Hong Kong is already showing signs of great progress. China is investing in Hong Kong, and the outlines of the colossal Bank of China building which stands alongside the Hongkong and Shanghai headquarters built by private capitalism may be seen as a symbol of the new interest.

Will China take advantage of its opportunity? If it plays its hand shrewdly it would use the Hong Kong market to raise capital and interest investors in wider Chinese activities. It will learn from Hong Kong, annexing not only the territory but also something of its entrepreneurial spirit and belief in the market place. If China is less wise she will kill

Hong Kong by neglect or ignorance. The success of Hong Kong is based on people. There are no natural resources in the tiny colony. Money is made by offering services and by building markets. The people can leave just as easily as they came and many are now establishing alternative nationality elsewhere in case the annexation by China turns out to be heavy-handed. Hong Kong is worried not only by the draining of skilled people away from the colony as they flee in fear of China, but also by the large movement into the colony of Vietnamese boat people hoping that its streets are still paved with gold and with political freedoms. It is difficult at this stage to predict the outcome.

A worry for the Chinese regime is the strong pull of the periphery against the centre. The pace of change and advance is very different in different provinces. It is at its speediest in Canton nearest to Hong Kong, at its slowest in the far north west of China. China throughout its imperial past had difficulties in keeping together such large and disparate peoples. The experiment with markets has run into some technical economic difficulties. The communist regime clamped the massive inflation of the pre-communist era and by a system of quotas and rationing kept prices under good control for more than 40 years of its rule. Now that it is introducing market pressures again, it has released a rapid inflation which is causing considerable difficulty.

The reformers say that the inflation can be handled. There will be a supply side response to the big surge in demand which in due course will bring prices under control. They also point to the possible need for a more disciplined banking and money market system along western lines so that the amount of credit in the economy can be brought under some kind of control. The Conservatives argue that it just shows that flirting with capitalism is dangerous. They see inflation, unemployment and bankruptcies as necessary corollaries of the capitalist system, and undesirable ones which it is better to live without. They argue strongly for a return to an ordered poverty rather than a disorderly and diversified prosperity.

In Russia a similar problem has emerged in that a large gap has been created between what people now think they might be able to have and what the economy is able to deliver. It is easy to raise peoples' expectations: it is much more difficult to satisfy them. Growing links with the West, the deployment of western advertisements on Russian television, the travel of Russians to New York, London and Paris, the signs of some imported goods in certain select shops in the centres of the major cities are all things arousing strong consumer demands and preferences. At the moment neither the Russian nor the Chinese economy can deliver. Russia has both to grow its economy more quickly and divert resources from defence into consumption. But can Russia really convert her swords into ploughshares?

The centripetal forces are also more powerful in the Russian empire. In welcoming *glasnost* and the structural reforms of Mikhail Gorbachev I concentrated in the first edition on their likely economic impact. It is now possible to see a large political problem emerging. When an autocrat ordains that people shall be free, at first they do not believe him. When they do begin to believe, they start to express their freedom and their enthusiasm for independence in ways not entirely of his choosing or liking. I am sure that Mikhail Gorbachev foresaw the need for change, driven by economic necessity, as he realised just how far behind the West the Soviet Union had fallen. Yet one of the strongest reactions to the spirit of *glasnost* has come in the eastern European satellites where rampant nationalism is reviving fast.

It was always likely that in countries like Hungary, Poland and the Baltic States of Estonia, Latvia and Lithuania, the response to *glasnost* would be fastest if it were allowed. The three Baltic States have shown just how independent of Russia they still feel and how much they resent Russian attempts to impose rule from Moscow and to change the mix of populations. The dispute has resulted in an amended constitution which gives Moscow new centralising powers whilst trying to find a compromise on regional loyalties. Gorbachev had to resort to 'special forms of administration' to quell the revolts in Azerbaijan. The people who wished to turn to Armenia and Moscow needed to stop the rot quickly. These special forms of administration can now be imposed at will against any of the individual republics. Is it possible to have economic liberalism and greater freedom within the confines of a unified Russian state? How far can Mr Gorbachev allow the eastern European satellites to break free in spirit before the conservatives at home force him to respond or before he himself loses patience?

The problem is also acute in Poland, the country in eastern Europe that has gone furthest this time in building a genuine political opposition. Whilst the reforms throughout the Russian empire favouring choice of candidates in elections and allowing some limited amount of dissension in debate have been slow moving, in Poland an unorthodox opposition has gathered momentum of greater weight and importance. The combination of the Solidarity trade union movement and the Roman Catholic Church is providing a focus for serious opposition to the Polish Communist Party. Margaret Thatcher's visit to Poland in October 1988 showed just how intense the feelings are. She was welcomed with great affection by the shipyard workers of Gdansk, for they saw her not as the representative of a government that had to close uneconomic shipyards, but as a representative of a vital democratic tradition where opposition to government policy is encouraged and where there is freedom of expression. They sought to use her as a mediator with their government to try and encourage discussions which would lead to the creation of a genuine Polish political opposition.

In Hungary too advances have been made in the development of both official and unofficial opposition. There are those who fear the twelve yearly cycle. In 1956 Russia marched in on Hungary. In 1968 Russia marched in on Czechoslavakia. In 1980 Russia marched in on Poland. Will 1992 see a recurrence of the twelve yearly pattern? Which state this time will be in the firing line? Will it have been the Baltic States that have gone too far in trying to secede or will Hungary or Poland once again have overstepped the mark?

Any observer must now recognise that the future of Europe is much less certain than at any time since 1939 with strong centralising forces now under attack from the twin forces of political dissent and rampant nationalism.

Moves to free the market places of the world continue apace. Several critics of the first edition have referred to the absence of comment in the book on the wider European Community. This was deliberate, as most of the advances being made in the field of deregulation and the creation of broader markets were being taken by national governments. The British deregulation and privatisation movement owed nothing to Brussels. Movements elsewhere beyond the confines of Europe mirrored the British experience without needing briefing from the European Commission.

Since the first edition was written there has been a quickening of pace towards the creation of a single European market by 1992. The impact of the Single European Act and majority voting, coupled with a defined aim of removing the barriers to trade throughout the twelve member states has had a beneficial impact in creating some reality out of the concept of Europe. The advances have been solid and workmanlike. The single administration document greatly simplifying the customs documentation needed to take containers and lorryloads of goods around the member states is a welcome improvement. The definition of common standards in a variety of areas and the mutual recognition of products from different countries around the market in others has speeded the possibility of greater internal trade within the EC. The embryo of a policy on EC mergers and acquisitions and the growing involvement of the European Court in a number of industrial and economic affairs is a further sign that Europe is gaining some tangible reality.

The European Community as currently constituted represents not only a possible means of extending the gains of wider and freer markets but also a potential threat. There are many in continental Europe who favour the concept of a fortress Europe. To them the benefits of the EC lie not so much in unrestricted trade between the member nations, as in substantial restrictions against trade from overseas, especially from Japan. The EC is actively discussing further obstacles in the way of Japanese finance houses investing in Europe and Japanese car manufacturers exporting their products into Europe. The Americans broadly welcome dealing with a single European power rather than a dozen separate countries, but they too are greatly concerned lest the European ideal of free trade is transmuted into a heavily defended fortress which prohibits American exports. The Rhodes Summit declaration against further barriers on external trade was a reassuring development.

As the European Community attempts to move on from building a single market to wider political involvement, there are fears that its response to changes in the East may send misleading signals or may become too feeble. Those European countries that wish to send subsidies and aid to Mikhail Gorbachev's regime at this early stage in the development of liberalisation are mistaken. Russia is still an autocracy, heavily armed and spending too much of its gross national product on weapons. Unless and until Russia is prepared to make a sizeable cut in its arms budgets and give some more political freedom to its subject peoples there is no case whatsoever for western Europe extending cash aid. Pumping more money into the corrupt and inefficient centralised state Russian system, far from giving help, will hinder. There is no shortage of potential demand in the Russian economy: the problem is the inefficiency of the supply side, resulting from monopolies, centralisation, corruption and the lack of incentive.

There remain great difficulties in creating a wider European ideal out of the important beginnings in the creation of the wider European market. Countries like Austria and Sweden that are wondering whether they should join are not interested in joining a defence union or a federal Europe: they do not want to miss out on a big free trade zone which might create greater prosperity. France and Ireland refuse in their different ways to co-operate with NATO. France intends to remain a separately armed independent power not committing its forces to the NATO alliance, whilst Ireland wishes to retain a strict neutrality concentrating its defence resources only on itself. This means that powers like Britain concerned that Europe, now rich, should make a bigger contribution to its own defence at a time when American budgets are under pressure, have to turn to the Western European Union as a possible way forward in developing more joint defence commitments between most of the major European powers.

Good European statesmanship now requires concentration on the strategic objectives of genuine deregulation and freedom throughout the western European market, on continuing progress through GATT to make sure that the advantages of free trade are spread well beyond the boundaries of Europe, and diligence to keep western Europe's guard up at a time of dramatic change in eastern Europe. These three policies together could ensure that western Europe does not get into crises with Japan and the United States nor encourage the impoverishment of the world by competitive devaluations, subsidies and protection between the major trading blocs. They could ensure that the western European economies continue to be a model for economic liberalism which Mikhail Gorbachev will have to follow, conscious as he is of how far the Soviet Union is falling behind. Maintaining the pressure for disarmament by keeping up western Europe's guard is also the surest way of delivering the large weapons reductions which we wish to see without jeopardising the West's security. It would be foolish to become so enamoured of the new Soviet style approach to western Europe that we gave away our weapons long before we could be sure that the new regime in Russia is permanent or that its intentions are entirely honourable.

The West has to be particularly watchful about the role of West Germany. There are many politicians in West Germany who are looking to Russia and thinking of the possibility of German reunification. Given the way that Russia suffered in two world wars at the hands of Germany it is extremely unlikely that Russia would in the end connive at the reunification of Germany, creating a massive economic power in the centre of the European continent. However, Mikhail Gorbachev's diplomatic shrewdness is such that he will dangle the prospect of improved contacts and greater co-operation between East and West Germany as a device to try and detach Germany from the full NATO alliance. Now is the time for Britain to sound warning notes and to make sure that the western European wider, freer economic market does not become conjoint with a sell out to Russia in the east.

Elsewhere in the world similar moves are underway to create freer markets. The Canadian election in November of 1988 took the form of a referendum on free trade in the north American continent. The ruling Conservative Party favoured the full free trade agreement with the United States of America, arguing that an open frontier would create greater prosperity. The Liberal opposition appealed to Canadian nationalism, saying that Mr Mulrooney, the Prime Minister, wished to sell out Canadian interests to the United States of America and wished to turn

Canada into the fifty first state of the union. It was a close-fought battle and showed just how emotional the issues of free trade and nationalism can become, especially when they pull in opposite directions. The open market won and further progress is now being made in pulling down barriers along the 49th parallel.

There is an opportunity for further superpower disarmament, given the financial problems of the United States of America. The new President, President Bush, inherits President Reagan's enthusiasm for negotiating major disarmament from strength. The United States of America needs to bring its federal deficit under more control, and the main area of spending is, of course, the defence budget. If America were able to get a verifiable agreement to cut out further categories of weaponry it might be possible to reduce American expenditure. This would suit the Russians as they desperately try to free resources to match some of the rising expectations of their people.

In The Road to Ruin (chapter 3), I set out the growing problem of debt in many parts of the world. The oil crisis debt, followed by Third World debt had shaken the foundations of many leading banking institutions. Unfortunately at the very point where banks are beginning to right their balance sheets by raising new equity, by writing down some of the bad advances and being more prudent about lending to difficult parts of the world, another debt crisis seems to be in the making. The last few years have seen an explosion in junk bonds. These are used to pay for mega mergers. The US marketplace has produced a series of entrepreneurial raiders, mounting ever larger bids for ever larger companies, with bigger and bigger proportions of debt to equity. A defence mechanism against the raider has often been a similarly heavily leveraged purchase by the managers and employees of the company itself.

All the normal rules of prudent banking seem to have been thrown out of the window in some of the more spectacular deals. Managements have been prepared to take on billions of dollars of debt. Deals have reached levels of leverage where nine-tenths of all the capital involved in the transaction is borrowed and only one-tenth is equity. People have discovered that heavily leveraged deals can produce massive profits when everything goes well. Of course if equity is only one-tenth of the total deal and the profits double, the return on equity is astonishingly good. What people seem to have forgotten is that things can go wrong, and that if they do the losses will be equally spectacular.

The whole leveraged buy-out and management buy-out movement, using debt, has been predicated on a continuing bull market, on continuing growth in underlying product and service markets and continuing opportunities to sell unneeded assets at ever higher prices. It is a game of pass the parcel where as long as you can see a way of selling the company on in two or three years' time at a profit, you are happy to do the deal. In the process, the managers may help to wreck the company they have bought. They will slash the capital spending, cut out the research and development, cut the training budget, reduce the work-force, push the prices up as far as they will go in the short term, all in the interests of maximising cash flow into the business. Then a year or two later they hope to sell it on with a stronger cash flow apparent from the figures at an ever higher multiple. In the end this process will be self-destructive, because companies will have built nothing for the future. If too much of the capital investment programme is cut, there will not be modern production facilities. If all the R & D is stopped, there will be no new ideas for the markets of the future. If spending on people and training is reduced too far, the life blood of the business will go.

More serious is the possibility that at some point in the next few years, growth may slow down or a recession could occur. In these conditions the heavily leveraged deals will look sick. Instead of profits increasing they will decrease. Then the interest burden will be crippling in relation to the reduced profitability, and some businessmen may find themselves in the bankruptcy courts.

It is not universal gloom around the world. In the United Kingdom the government is now showing how a country can do what many banks have done, and build up its equity and get out of debt. This year will see an estimated financial surplus of £10,000 million in the United Kingdom public sector. Against a total outstanding public debt of £160 billion, this represents a sizeable repayment of outstanding obligations. Were the government to continue to run this level of surplus for the next three years, which is quite feasible, one fifth of the total national debt could have been repaid. The advantages of deregulation, faster growth and fiscal prudence are now coming through in this dramatic surplus now being generated.

The chapter on privatisation pointed to how the message was spreading across the seas. Progress continues to be rapid in many parts of the world. In the United Kingdom, the home of privatisation, a series of crucial decisions has been taken to advance the cause still further. Towards the end of 1988 the British Steel industry was returned to the private sector. The transformation in British Steel's fortunes was dramatic. Less than ten years earlier the Corporation had been losing £1,000 million a year and was the least efficient of any of the mainstream producers around the world. Today it is a highly profitable business where the productivity record is not only better than that of the Germans but also better than that of the Japanese.

More important than the privatisation of British Steel has been the decision to move ahead with the privatisation of the major public utility monopoly, the electricity industry. The active debate foreshadowed in the first edition of the book over how electricity should be privatised has resulted in a scheme which favours a major strengthening of competitive forces. The privatisation has worked on the proposition that eight-tenths of the total cost of producing electricity to the final consumer are incurred in the generating process. Generating electricity is not a natural monopoly in a sizeable country. In order to make it competitive the Central Electricity Generating Board's generating capacity is being split into two separate companies, Power Gen and National Power. At the same time the Scottish industry will be privatised separately and will be able to sell its power across the border into England as a third competitive force. A fourth competitive force comes in the form of the 2000 megawatt link across the Channel to France, allowing the importation of French power from its nuclear generation system. The fifth competitive force will come from those private companies who take advantage of the deregulated regime in order to establish their own power production and link in to the central grid. This model for privatising a utility through the introduction of substantial competition is likely to be one which is followed widely overseas as governments turn to looking at utilities as well as at their competitive businesses.

The Jamaican programme is advancing well. Since the sale of Caribbean Cement the government has announced further privatisations and has succeeded in selling a major stake in its Telephone Company. The privatisation of the Jamaican Telephone Company is an example of how developing country privatisations can strengthen the position of a company and a government at the same time. A stake was sold to Cable & Wireless, the British multinational company with substantial experience of operating telephone systems around the world. This sale included raising some new monies in the form of hard currency, much needed by the Jamaican Telephone Company as part of its re-equipment programme. A second tranche of shares was sold to the employees and the wider Jamaican public in an offer for sale. For this offering the Jamaican Government pioneered underwriting in the Jamaican stock market, using it for the first time in a Jamaican public issue. The sale went extremely smoothly and the whole issue was underwritten just before the hurricane hit the island. It is a testimony to the robustness of privatisation, the stock market and the new underwriting system that they all survived the hurricane with flying colours. The selling programme went ahead and the Jamaican public responded well, leaving the underwriters without a single share. The third shareholding remains in the hands of the government so they too retain a partnership interest in the Jamaican telephone system.

In Canada some of the provinces are looking more actively at privatisation. The Province of Saskatchewan is particularly active, attempting to rebuild its programme after an unsuccessful sale of an energy company at a time of falling oil prices. One of the ways of rejuvenating the programme has been the development of the Saskatchewan power bond. This is the sale of an ordinary bond to fixed-interest investors, but it has attached to it the right to convert the bond into shares at a future date. If this occurs, it will be the first example of a deferred privatisation taking place some years after the initial sale with the conversion of a fixed-interest instrument into a voting instrument.

Rescheduling and debt swap also continue to make rapid progress. There is a better market now in much Third World debt. Many major banks are still busily writing down their positions, although it is proving more difficult to get the international organisations like the World Bank to accept the same medicine. UK Chancellor Nigel Lawson's sub Saharan debt initiative has been most helpful in getting other countries to agree with Britain to write off the debt of the poorest African states as there is no serious possibility of this debt ever being repaid. The precarious balancing act with Latin American debt, especially Brazilian, Argentinian and Mexican, continues between the borrowers and the lenders. The Baker plan has not been a wild success, in that there are few examples of Third World countries whose growth has suddenly taken off as a result of the application of its principles. However, without something like it, without the acknowledgment that growth was an important part of the remedy for the Third World debt crisis, it is very likely that the crisis would have been much more intense, and the western banks would have found it difficult to handle wholesale reneging on obligations. The power of the yen continues to build up and the yen is gradually displacing the dollar as the world's leading reserve currency. More and more banking business is being written in yen, and the Japanese banks are coming to recognise ever greater obligations to lend around the world as Japan continues to be the one strong surplus country capable of taking the strain in a period of American eclipse.

Stock exchanges have been battered by the events of the crash in the autumn of 1987. Yet one of the remarkable things is that stock exchanges are still capable of raising substantial sums of money for major issues and placings despite the dent to optimism administered by the sharp fall in share prices in September and October of 1987. Immediately after the crash London was able to raise substantial sums of money needed for the Channel Tunnel. It has gone on to handle steel privatisation and can look forward to the major electricity privatisation without any great difficulty. The tussle between regulation and freedom still remains unresolved. There is recognition in London that the complicated rule book, written as a result of the Financial Services Act, did go far too far in trying to lay down detailed regulations. A new head of the Security and Investment Board has come in pledged to greatly simplify the rule book and reduce it to 100 basic principles. As this work proceeds there is some optimism in London that the climate for business may improve as a result of doing away with many of the detailed regulations.

Tax reform is on the worldwide agenda. The Japanese have just put through major proposals to cut rates of taxation on income and to impose a modest sales tax. Japan accepts the logic of switching taxation away from income towards spending, to encourage enterprise and saving and to make sure that the spread of taxation is fair at a time when the population is ageing rapidly. More countries are likely to take action to simplify and cut direct taxes as they see the galvanising result it has had in the United States and in the United Kingdom. The enterprise culture in the United Kingdom continues to expand rapidly. Urban development, stimulated by development corporations, is now in full swing in many northern and western cities as well as within the London Docklands area. Birmingham is at the centre of a construction boom. Manchester is beginning to prosper, and even in places as far north as Newcastle activity is speeding up noticeably. Industry is responding to the growing costs and congestion of the South East and to the growing sense of purpose and enthusiasm of the North West and North East. The UK manufacturing industry, for so long in the doldrums, is also showing signs of greatly improved performance. In the early 1980s, during the recession, it learned the lesson about the need to control costs and to raise productivity. In the later 1980s it is having to learn the equally hard lesson that good business also rests upon the recruitment, retention and training of high calibre people, upon supporting innovation, new processes and new products, and upon reinvesting in adequate and new production facilities. All this is now beginning to happen, but so much more remains to be done as manufacturing is still the weakest of the principal sectors of the United Kingdom economy.

The main conclusions of the book have been underlined by events of the last eighteen months. There is a worldwide movement towards democracy and towards greater economic freedom. The results of these two processes are likely to be benign. Asia is swept by democratic revolutions, Latin America is gingerly stepping out from autocracy and trying to get out from under the weight of its debt. Europe is the melting pot where the economic culture of 1992 jostles with experiments in freedom in the eastern European bloc.

The US and Japan are trying to adjust to their altered roles, with Japan having to take on the mantle of the reserve currency and principal bankers to the world. The Americans are slowly having to reduce the scale of their overseas role, at first through the private sector and now through the public sector, as they recognise the limits to expansion based on debt. I am still optimistic about the likely progress of economic liberalism, privatisation and deregulation. I am more cautious about the future of the European Community, where it is important that forces for freedom triumph over forces for intervention and bigger government. I am also worried about developments in the Balkans and the Baltic States. It will require western statesmanship of a high order now that the Russian experiment is coming under pressure. The opportunity for change is greater than ever. The chance for it to miscarry is also now greater.

Index

aid, economic 69
Aims of Industry 146
airlines and airports 76-7, 81-2,
    85-6, 88-9, 152
Alfa Romeo 78-9
alienation 32
Amersham International 38, 72,
    83-4, 86
Aquino, Corazon 20-3, 35-6,
    156
Arab states 46-7
Argentina 6, 23, 80
Associated British Ports 83, 86
Austin-Rover 79
Australia 33, 139
Austria 35, 80

Baker Plan vii, 68
Bank of America 64-5
Bank of England 102, 121
Bank of Montreal 65-6
Bank of Tokyo 64
banking 46-70, 114
    bad debts 59, 62-3
    Canada 59, 65-6, 71
    cost of lending 62-7
    debt swap and 101
    debts and capital flight 55-9
    eurobonds 46
    growth and recycling 50-5
    institutions 51-2
    Japan 52, 59, 61-2
    laws and rules 51, 60
    mortgages 125-6
    new equity 64-5
    oil money 46-8
    privatisation of 73-6, 89
    reserves 63-6
    technology for recovery
        67-70
    UK 65, 125-6
    USA 51-3, 59-65
Barclays Bank 64
Belgium 80
Bell Company 29

Boeing 36, 73
Bolivia 99
Boyson, Rhodes 146
Brand Report vii
Brazil 6-7, 23, 67, 70, 80, 100
British Aerospace 72, 82-3, 85,
    87
British Airports Authority 85-6
British Airways 77, 82-4, 88
British Broadcasting
    Corporation 89
British Columbia Resources
    and Investment Corporation
    71
British Gas, 39, 78, 82-3, 85,
    92, 124
British Leyland 79, 82,84
British National Freight
    Corporation 38, 72, 83-4,
    156
British National Oil
    Corporation 38, 85
British Petroleum (BP) 71-2,
    82-3, 86, 124, 130-1
British Rail 82, 107
British Shipbuilders 82
British Sugar Corporation 83
British Telecom
    competition for 29, 90-1
    decision to privatise 72-3,
        120, 146
    impact of privatisation
        123-4, 147
    opposition to privatisation
        38-9, 122
    planning for privatisation
        120-2
    price control 91
    proceeds from 83, 85
    share issue 123-5, 132
Britoil 83, 85-6
Broakes, Nigel 143
building societies 125-6
bureaucracy 44
Business Expansion Scheme 137

businesses, small 11, 15-16, 30,
134, 152

Cable and Wireless Company
38, 82-4, 86
Canada
banks 59, 65-6
privatisation 36-7, 71, 73-4,
148
Canadian Imperial Bank of
Commerce 66
capital, flight of 57-9
capitalism 26, 153-4
see also popular capitalism
car industry 78-9, 82, 84-5, 104
Caribbean Cement 87
Cellnet 90
censorship 2
Channel Tunnel project 28,
107-8
Chase Manhattan Bank 52,
63-4
Chemical Bank 64
Chile 23, 80, 94, 99-101, 151
China, People's Republic of
agriculture 8, 9
communism 7-8
industry 11, 12
markets 9-10, 12, 155
privatisation 11-12
project finance 111
stock markets 12, 153
Chirac, Jacques 73, 87, 149
Chun, Mr 7
Citi-Corp 52, 62-5
cities 42-3, 140-4
Clydesdale Bank 65
communism 7-8, 26
see also Marxism
Compagnie Générale
d'Electricité 88
Conrail 82
Conservative Party, UK
and liberalisation 37-9
and privatisation 72, 79,
82-7, 90-2, 120-5, 146-8
and stock market 118, 128-9
and taxation 30-1, 134-8
Continental Illinois Bank 60
Crédit Commercial de France 88

Crédit Suisse 64

Dai-Ichi Bank 62, 64
Dartford Tunnel project 150-1
debt
investment 68-70
market solution 93-4, 151-2,
154
rescheduling 56, 93-4, 98
Third World (*q.v.*) 50-1,
54-6, 67-70, 93
debt swap 29, 67, 93-102, 105,
151-2
banks and 101
Jamaica 96-8
mechanism 94-6
privatisation 98-9
problems 101-2
deflation 53
De Havilland 36, 73
democracy 1-23, 154-6
communism and 7-8, 9-12
economy and 2-3, 23
Europe 4-6
failure of 2-3
Korea 7
Latin America 6-7
market mechanism and 8-9
Philippines 20-3
USSR reforms 13-19
Deng Xiao-Ping 8
Deutschebank 64
developing countries *see* Third
World
dictatorships 1-2, 5-6, 23
Dole, Mrs 81
Douglas, Roger 33-4, 77
Downer, Richard 74-6

Ecuador 67
Egan, John 84
electricity 78, 92, 111-12
energy 8-9, 47-8
see also oil; utilities
ENI, Spain 78-9
Enterprise Oil 83, 85-6
equity 132
conversions to 64-5, 67
investment 67-70, 114-15
see also stock markets

Ethiopia 2
eurobonds 46, 52, 61, 152
exchange controls 58, 105

Falkland Islands war 6, 37
Fiat 78-9
Fiji 23
Financial Services Act, UK 129
Finland 35, 89-90
Ford Motor Company 79
France
    democracy 4
    liberalisation 35
    privatisation 73, 87-9, 124,
        148-9
    stock market 30, 130, 132
    taxation 136
    unemployment 43, 139
freedom, political and economic
    2-3, 23, 155-6
Fuji Bank 64

General Motors 79
Germany 4, 80, 139
Glass-Steagall rules, USA 60
Gorbachev, Mikhail 13-19, 155
government *see* state
Greece 5
growth, economic
    and liberalisation 41-2
    and recycling 50-5
    Third World 48, 50, 66
Guthrie Corporation 76

Havas 88
Hawke, Bob 33
Hayek, F.A. von 53
Heath, Edward 145
Herstatt Bank 60
Hungary 11

incentives 10, 15-16, 32, 133
India 3
industrial relations 145, 147-8
industry
    declining 140-1
    nationalised 24-5, 48-50,
        156
    privatisation 11, 12, 78-9,
        82-6

see also motor; small
    businesses; telecommuni-
    cations; *etc.*
inequalities 34, 42, 139-42
inner cities 42-3, 140-4
insider trading 127, 129
Institute of Economic Affairs 146
insurance, life 126-7, 137
international bonds 60
International Monetary Fund
    (IMF) 58, 68, 71-2, 94,
    96-8, 100
investment 114-15, 152-3
    debt 68-70
    equity 69-70
    foreign, direct 103-6
    liquidity 115
    pension funds 126-7
    tax 134-5, 137
    see also stock markets
IRI, Italy 78-9, 89
Italy 4, 78-9, 139, 148

Jaguar cars 82, 84
Jamaica
    debt swap 96-8
    privatisation 74-6, 87, 89,
        149
    stock market 131-2
Japan
    and economic recession
        138-9
    and oil 47
    banks 52, 59, 61-2
    car industry 104
    foreign direct investment 104
    industry 11, 104
    privatisation 77, 88, 124
    stock market 116, 130, 132,
        153
    unemployment 43
Japan Airlines 88
Joseph, Sir Keith 146

Kim, Mr 7
King, Lord 84
KLM 77, 88

Labour Party, UK 38-40, 71-2,
    122

Lange, David 33-4
Latin America
  debts 63-4, 67-8, 151
  democracy 6-7
  privatisation 80
laws and rules
  banking 51, 60
  financial trading 127-31,
    153-4
Liberal Party, UK 38-41
liberalisation of industry and
    commerce 24-45
  Australia 33
  Canada 36-7
  capitalism 25-7
  competition 29
  debt swap 29, 93-102
  division 34
  Europe 34-5, 43
  government role and 24-5
  growth and 41-2
  mobility and 42-3
  New Zealand 33-4, 43-4
  Philippines 35-6
  political opposition 33, 38-41
  privatisation (*q.v.*) 28
  project financing 28, 106-12
  small businesses 30
  stock markets 29-30, 114-32
  taxation (*q.v.*) 30-1, 132-44
  UK 27-9, 37-43
  unemployment and 43-4
life insurance 126-7, 137
Lloyds Bank 64
Loi Monory 30, 130, 136
London Docklands Development
    Corporation 141-4
London Stock Exchange 30,
    116-23, 130-2
  British Telecom sale 120-3
  laws and rules 127-30
  reforms 118-19

McDougall, Barbara 74
McFadden rules, USA 60
McLeod Young Weir 121
Malaysia 76, 103-4
Manufacturers' Hanover Bank
    63-5
Marcos, Ferdinand 20-2

markets 8-10, 12, 24
  see also stock markets
Marx, Karl 26, 32
Marxism 1-2, 25-7, 45
  see also Union of Soviet
    Socialist Republics
MAS 88
media 89, 153
Mellish, Bob 143
Mercury 29, 90
Mexico 67, 93-4, 99-101, 151
Midland Bank 64-5
military régimes 1, 5-6, 23
Mitterrand, François 35, 73,
  148
mobility 42
monopolies 24-5, 27-8
  see also liberalisation
Morgan Guarantee Trust 57-8,
  64
Morgan Stanley and Company
  121
Morrison, Herbert 48-50
motor industry 78-9, 82, 84-5,
  104
multinational corporations 52,
  104, 106

National Australia Bank 65
National Bus Company 27-8,
  86
National Commercial Bank of
  Jamaica 74-6, 89, 149
National Enterprise Board 83
National Freight Corporation
  38, 72, 83-4, 156
National Investment Bank of
  Jamaica 74-5
National Seed Development
  Council 86
National Westminster Bank 64
nationalised industry 24-5,
  48-50, 156
  see also privatisation
Netherlands 3
New Zealand
  economy 33-4, 157
  privatisation 77-8, 157
  stock market 127
  unemployment 43-4, 139, 142

Nippon Telephone and
  Telegraph 124
Nomura Bank 61-2, 121
North Sea Oil Licences 83
Northern Bank 65
Northern Bank of Ireland 65

Office of Fair Trading 118
oil
  financing 112
  prices 8-9, 47
  privatisation 83-6
  producers 46-7
  use of 47-8
opposition, political, to
  liberalisation
  Australia 33
  UK 38-41, 71-2, 122
Organisation for Economic
  Co-operation and Development (OECD) 103
Owen, David 39

Paribas 88-9
Parkinson, Cecil 118
pensions 126-7, 136
Peru 67, 89
Peter I, the Great, Emperor of
  Russia 19
Petrocorp 78
Philippines
  debt swap 96, 101, 151
  democracy 20-3, 156
  economy 35-6, 132
Pinochet, General August 23
popular capitalism 31-2, 44-5,
  132, 155-7
  banking 46-70
  democracy 1-23
  liberalisation 24-45, 146-55
  privatisation 71-92
  stock markets 114-32
  taxation 132-44
  technology, financial
    93-113
Portugal 4-5, 34-5, 89
price mechanism 8-9, 24
Price Waterhouse 75
privatisation 28, 71-92, 148-50
  banking 71, 74-6, 89

Canada 36-7, 71, 73-4
  debt swap 98-9
  Finland 89-90
  France 73, 87-9, 124, 148-9
  Italy 78-9
  Jamaica 74-6, 87, 89
  Japan 77, 88, 124
  Latin America 80, 89
  New Zealand 33-4, 77-8
  Philippines 35-6
  Portugal 35, 89
  South-east Asia 76
  Spain 78-9
  taxation and 136
  telecommunications 72-3,
    84, 90-1, 120-5, 146-7
  transport 76-7, 81-6, 88-9,
    146, 152
  UK 37-9, 72, 79, 82-7, 90-2,
    120-5, 146-8
  USA 73, 81-2
  utilities 78, 82-3, 85, 92, 124
Prodi, Professor 78-9
projects, private financing of
  28, 106-12, 149
  mechanism 108-10
  risks 112
  Turkey 110-11
  UK 28, 107-8, 111-12,
    149-51
  utilities 111-12

Racal Vodafone 90
recovery, economic
  enterprise and 138-44
  financial technology for
    67-70, 97-113
Redwood, John 74-6
rescheduling, debt 56, 93-4, 98
Rolls Royce 85
Rothschilds, N.M. viii, 75
Royal Ordnance 85

Saint Gobain 88
Salomon Inc. 62, 64
savings *see* investment
Scargill, Arthur 145-6
Sealink 82
Seat 79

Securities and Exchange
  Commission, USA 129
Schultz, George 73
Singapore Airlines 88
small businesses 11, 15-16, 30,
  134, 152
Social Democratic Party, UK
  39-41
Société Générale 88
South Africa 108-9
South Korea 7, 11, 22, 111
Southeast Asia
  democracy 7, 20-3
  foreign investment in 106
  privatisation 76, 88
  project financing 111
Spain 4, 78-9, 139, 148
state
  controls 4
  enterprise and recovery
    138-44
  industry ownership 24-5,
    48-50, 156
  role of 24-5
  stock market and 118,
    128-9
  taxation (*q.v.*) 30-1, 132-44
  see also laws; liberalisation;
    privatisation
stock markets 114-32, 153
  Chile 80-1
  China 12, 153
  development of 29-30,
    114-16
  institutional dominance of
    125-7
  laws and rules 127-30, 153-4
  privatisation and 120-5
  reforms 118-19
  technology and 117-19, 153
strikes 145, 147-8
Suarez, Mario 35
Suez 88
Sumitomo Bank 62
Swiss Bank Corporation 121
syndicated bank loans 60

taxation 30-1, 132-44
  corporation 31, 134-5
  income 31, 134

investment 134-5, 137
  pensions and life insurance
    126-7, 136
  reform of 134-8
  reliefs 133, 136
  simplification of 134-5,
    138
  UK 134-8
Taylor Woodrow 143
technology 51
  and stock markets 117-19,
    153
  financial 67-70, 97-113
    debt swap 93-102
    foreign direct investment
      103-6
    project financing 106-12
    rescheduling 56, 93
telecommunications
  competition 29, 42, 90
  nationalisation 50
  privatisation 72-3, 84, 90-1,
    120-5, 146-7
TFI (TV) 88
Thatcher, Margaret 19, 33,
  37-8, 71, 155
Third World
  aid to 69
  borrowing 50-1, 54-5,
    59-60, 67-70, 93, 151
  capital flight 57-9
  debt swaps 93-102, 151-2
  dictatorships 1-2
  foreign direct investment
    103-6
  market solution 93-4, 151-2,
    154
  nationalised industry 48-50
  push for growth 48, 50, 66
  stock markets 130, 132
Toronto Dominion Bank 66
trades unions 145, 147-8
transport 152
  liberalisation 27-8
  nationalisation 49-50
  privatisation 77, 82-5, 146
  projects 107-8
Turkey 5, 110-11, 131, 148

unemployment 43-4, 139

Union of Soviet Socialist
  Republics
  agriculture 9, 16-17
  and UK 19
  dissent 10
  economy 8, 155
  ideology 17-18
  markets 9-10, 12
  reforms 13-19, 155
United Kingdom (UK)
  and USSR 19
  banks 65, 125-6
  cities 42-3, 140-4
  Conservative Party 37-8,
    71-2
  democracy 156
  Empire and free trade 3
  enterprise and recovery 140-4
  exchange controls 105
  growth 41-2
  nationalisation 48-50
  opposition, political 38-41,
    71-2, 122
  privatisation 37-9, 72, 79,
    82-7, 90-2, 120-5, 146-8
  projects 28, 107-8, 111-12,
    149-51
  regional variations 139-41
  stock market 30, 114-23,
    153-4

strikes 145, 147-8
taxation 31, 126-7, 134-8
telecommunications 29, 42,
  120-5, 146-7
transport 27-8, 82-5, 146
unemployment 43-4, 139
utilities 83, 85, 92, 111-12
United States of America
  (USA)
  banks 51-3, 59-65
  debts 53-4
  democracy 3
  Federal Reserve 59, 64,
    102
  privatisation 73, 81-2
  recession 53, 139
  stock market 116-17, 124,
    127, 129-30, 132, 153
  taxation 31, 135-6, 138
  telecommunications 29
  unemployment 43, 139
utilities 50
  privatisation 78, 83, 85, 92
  project financing 111-12

Vargasllosa, Mario 89
Volkswagen 79

Washington airports 81-2
World Bank 11, 94, 96-8